Tom Barry is co-director of the Resource Center. Deb Preusch, also a director of the Resource Center, was the main researcher for the report. The author is especially grateful for the excellent editing by Beth Wood. The Resource Center is also grateful to Reggie Norton of the Washington Office on Latin America (WOLA) and Bob Stix of the Network in Solidarity with Guatemala (NISGUA) for reading and commenting on the manuscript. Cover and layout design by Judith Kidd with assistance from Jack Kutz. Sally Gwylan managed the word processing, and Kathy Schwartz helped with layout. Photographs by Tom Barry.

Copyright © by the Inter-Hemispheric Education Resource Center.

All rights reserved.

No part of this booklet may be reproduced, stored in a retrieval system, or transmitted in any form, by any means, including mechanical, electronic, photocopying, recording, or otherwise, without prior written permission of the publisher.

First Printing 1986

Second Printing 1986

ISBN: 0-911213-06-6

CONTENTS

roduction	1
er the Coup: Designing the Showcase	5
ian Rebellion and Counterinsurgency	17
ification: A Joint Effort	41
temala: What Next?	80
erence Notes	97

Tables, Maps, & Diagrams

temala	i
allel Government	9
es of Development	32
nja Transversal del Norte	35
ir Years of Pacification	40
Military and Economic Aid to Guatemala 1949-1987	42
) to the Guatemalan Government	48
tilateral Assistance to the Guatemalan Government	51
rld Food Program Assistance	53
) Assistance	67
Economic and Military Assistance to the Guatemalan Government	69
nilarities Between US Economic Aid Projects and the Army's Security and Development Plan	74

Introduction

> Our economic aid "is directed at the rural poor, especially the Indians" and "addresses the underlying social/economic conditions which fan insurgency."
>
> -- Peter McPherson, Administrator, Agency for International Development, 1983.

In January 1986 political power in Guatemala passed from military to civilian hands. President Reagan hailed this "democratization" as a triumph for his foreign policy in Central America. In Guatemala, there was widespread hope that the inauguration of Vinicio Cerezo would bring an end to three decades of political bloodshed and military repression.

But the prospects for peace and broad democratization in Guatemala are not good. Instead it is likely that the politics of counterinsurgency will continue to dominate this Central American country. The politics of counterinsurgency have molded the internal affairs of Guatemala ever since 1954, the year a U.S.-directed military coup overthrew the reformist government of President Jacobo Arbenz. All attempts to institute reforms in land tenure and income distribution patterns have been labeled as communist-inspired and brutally crushed. And in the name of eliminating guerrilla movements, the military has terrorized the entire population.

In the last ten years, the politics of counterinsurgency have pervaded Guatemalan life as never before. Most of rural Guatemala is under military siege, and the army has extended its influence over an array of government ministries and public sector corporations. The new civilian government has taken office but has not taken over control of the country. Reforms necessary to truly change the country have been ruled out by the military high command and the country's business elite as well as by Vinicio Cerezo himself and the Christian Democrats. Without substantial reforms, insurgency and counterinsurgency will remain the major political forces in Guatemala.

This Resource Center report examines the origins and evolution of the politics of counterinsurgency in Guatemala. Particular attention is paid to the critical role played by the United States. The report focuses on the military's dual counterinsurgency strategy, which combines the iron fist of violence and repression with the velvet glove of pacification programs. The army calls this two-pronged approach its "security and development" plan.

SUMMARY OF FINDINGS

The report is based on numerous trips to Guatemala over the past several years by Tom Barry and Deb Preusch, the co-directors of the Resource Center. The results of this investigation of the politics of counterinsurgency in Guatemala can be summarized as follows:

* Since 1954 the United States has played a key role in developing the politics of counterinsurgency in Guatemala through its military and economic assistance programs.

* A great portion of the increased U.S. economic aid and the release of non-lethal military aid for the

highlands will be used to support the army's pacification campaign. This is particularly true of counterpart funds from large ESF and Title I food assistance.

* While many of the stated goals of the military's civic action, resettlement, and development programs are desirable, the programs actually serve to increase military control and block self-determined organization and development.

* The military's involvement or control of three key government organizations--Civil Affairs and Community Development (S-5), Inter-Institutional Coordination Committees (IICC), and the Committee of National Reconstruction (CRN)--allows it to manage rural development programs, especially in areas it calls areas of conflict.

* No significant development of the Indian highlands has resulted from the military's National Plan of Security and Development.

* The only visible sign of development in the highlands is the extensive construction of roads, whose primary function is increased military access to and control of this Indian-populated region.

* The army's pacification program has received most of its backing from international sources, the largest of which is the U.S. Agency for International Development (AID).

* AID has targeted virtually all its projects for the very areas targeted by the military for own pacification program.

* AID has backed the army's development poles and model villages through direct grants, counterpart

funding agreements, development assistance, and support of U.S. and Guatemalan Private Voluntary Organizations (PVOs).

* Rather than supporting grassroots peasant and community organizations, AID has put its money behind organizations tied to the military and the government.

* The army sponsored the 1984-85 electoral process as part of its long-range counterinsurgency plan adopted in 1982, and it is unlikely that it will allow the elected civilian government to take steps to demilitarize the conflict areas or weaken military institutions.

* AID has not used its economic assistance as leverage to push for reforms that directly tackle the distorted patterns of land ownership and income distribution.

* AID's economic development strategy for Guatemala and its ongoing policy dialogues with the government do not address the basic economic and political problems, but rather promote solutions that support the elite.

* The guerrilla movement will continue to exist because the new government will do nothing to substantially improve rural living conditions or reduce the militarization in the countryside.

After the Coup: Designing the Showcase

Security and development emerged as interrelated concerns after the 1954 CIA-backed coup that overthrew the progressive government of President Jacobo Arbenz. The coup ended a decade of civilian rule, which had begun when popular forces overthrew military dictator Jorge Ubico in 1944. From 1944 to 1954 Guatemala experimented with democracy and social reform. Two popularly elected presidents, Juan Jose Arevalo (1944-50) and Jacobo Arbenz (1951-54), launched a series of populist reforms, including a land redistribution program and laws safeguarding the right to organize. More than just cosmetic changes, the reforms cut into the wealth and power of the national oligarchy and the largest foreign investors.

President Arbenz in 1952 announced a modest agrarian reform program that caused serious repercussions in Washington. Among the landholdings expropriated and turned over to landless peasants by the program were the uncultivated estates of United Fruit. This angered several high government officials--including Secretary of State John Foster Dulles, CIA Director Allen Dulles, and UN Ambassador Henry Cabot Lodge--all of whom had business connections with United Fruit. United Fruit, with the help of the Eisenhower Administration, mounted a national propaganda campaign against Guatemala. The banana company paid writers to travel to Guatemala and publish articles in Readers Digest and other national magazines purporting to show that "international communism" was gaining a foothold in Central America. United Fruit's opinion of the developments in Guatemala were echoed in

Washington by cold-war warriors who saw little difference between the nationalism of the Arbenz government and the policies of the Soviet Union. The propaganda campaign against the Arbenz government culminated in 1954 when President Eisenhower authorized the CIA to plan and finance a military coup to overthrow the democratically elected government.[1]

The CIA selected Colonel Carlos Castillo Armas, vassal of the coffee oligarchy and extreme right wing, to lead the coup that pushed Arbenz into exile. Following the Armas takeover, the country experienced the first incidence of massive human rights violations in its recent history. In just 18 months, four thousand civilians were assassinated, and another 5,000 illegally detained and tortured.[2]

The Eisenhower Administration hailed the "liberation government" formed by Armas. Liberation from the communists was the theme of the CIA coup. It was also the slogan of a new right-wing party formed by Mario Sandoval Alarcon, the personal secretary of Castillo Armas, called the Movement for National Liberation (MLN)--a party that has since publicly associated itself with death squad operations. As the chief force behind the coup, the United States found itself caretaker of a military regime that had little popular support and no experience in government. Its survival depended on generous U.S. economic and technical assistance.

In the years after the coup, the country became a kind of pilot project for Washington. The post-1954 period in Guatemala provided Washington its first practical experience in using economic aid to stabilize and guide the development of a Latin American nation. On a visit to Guatemala to express official U.S. support for the new regime, Vice-President Richard Nixon declared that the 1954 coup was "the first instance where a Communist government has been replaced by a free one." He said, "The whole world is watching to see which does the better job."[3]

Journalist Freda Kirchway capsulized the situation in a 1954 article entitled "Guatemala Guinea Pig" that was printed in The Nation:

> Guatemala was chosen as a test case and a warning. The defeat of the Arbenz government, along with its supporters, has provided a sample of Washington's cold war strategy in the Western Hemisphere. As such it should be studied with care by other American states.[4]

The Eisenhower Administration announced that it intended to make Guatemala a "showcase of democracy." Using large sums of U.S. economic assistance and "know-how," it planned to turn Guatemala into a model for capitalist development throughout the hemisphere. While total foreign economic assistance to Guatemala amounted to only $2.5 million in the 1951-54 period, foreign economic aid totaled $101.2 million (including $18 million from the U.S.-controlled World Bank) from 1955 through 1958--a monumental gift considering that the total Latin American aid program averaged only $60 million a year during the same period.[5]

Dollars streamed into Guatemala City. "[The aid] flowed very, very rapidly....Practically overnight, I had $800,000 to spend," recalled one U.S. consultant.[6] President Armas told a U.S. reporter that if it had not been "for the technical and financial aid of the United States, it wouldn't have been possible to carry our program out."[7]

The U.S. International Cooperation Agency (ICA)--the predecessor of the Agency for International Development

(AID)--administered the economic aid program. Soon after the 1954 coup, ICA set up an office in Guatemala City. The mission grew from 28 employees in 1954 to 165 employees in 1959, including 94 U.S. citizens.[8] The ICA constituted what amounted to a parallel government in Guatemala. As a counterpart to each ministry and department of the Guatemalan government, ICA had its own coordinating office. The U.S. Information Service even published a schematic chart that illustrated the exact parallels between ICA divisions and Guatemalan ministries.[9] To polish the image of liberation government, ICA paid the salary of the president's public relations officer. Not only did ICA control the workings of the government's bureaucracy, it also tried to restructure the country's economy in ways that complemented the U.S.'s own economic interests. The agency promoted increased U.S. investment and encouraged increased cash-crop production.

A PARALLEL GOVERNMENT

Collaborating with ICA was the private consulting firm Klein and Saks (K&S), which specialized in "a prescription of private enterprise for the weak national economies" in the third world. K&S assisted ICA in rearranging almost every Guatemalan ministry, from the office of finance to the National Police.[10] A former K&S consultant reminisced: "The United States was almost in fact dictating the policies (of the government). Castillo Armas obeyed orders well." The 1955 Petroleum Law, which opened up the country to virtually uncontrolled mineral exploitation, was typical of the policies that resulted from ICA and K&S intervention.

The Armas government did pass a number of social programs, but they resulted in tighter social control instead of improvement of socioeconomic conditions. In the case of agrarian reform, ICA advisers supervised the dismantling of Arbenz's progressive land distribution

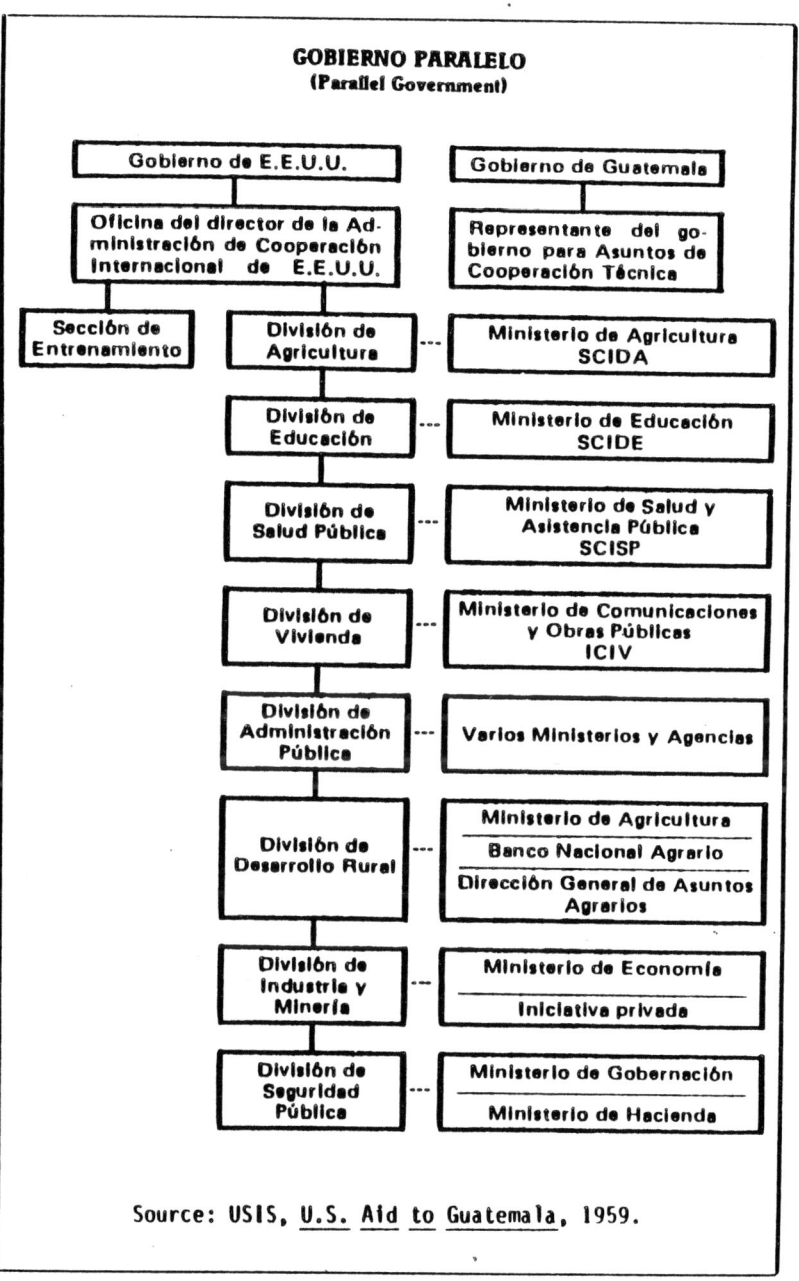

program. Estates were returned to the oligarchy, and 100,000 Guatemalans lost the plots of land they had gained under the civilian government. ICA did support nominal changes in land use, but catered to the elite's strong opposition of land reform and kept redistribution efforts at an insignificant level.

Despite U.S. economic aid and technical assistance, Guatemala did not become a shining model of democracy. By the time John F. Kennedy became president, Guatemala had become an embarrassment not a showcase. The 1954 coup had put the country back into the hands of the military and the oligarchy and paved the way for the formation of the national security state in Guatemala.

In 1963, President Kennedy foiled an easy opportunity in Guatemala to demonstrate the progressive principles of his Alliance for Progress. Former reformist president Juan Jose Arevalo announced his intention in 1962 to run for the presidency the following year. But political machinations by Washington and the Guatemalan military thwarted his hopes. The Kennedy Administration feared that an Arevalo victory would reduce U.S. influence in Guatemala. A January 1963 cable to the U.S. Embassy in Guatemala City from Undersecretary of State George Ball underscored this concern. It stated that "the Department considers Arevalo's return to power adverse to U.S. interests...."[11] Counting on U.S. backing, Defense Minister Enrique Peralta de Azurdia, warning of a new "communist danger," led a coup d'etat that blocked the scheduled elections and the expected Arevalo victory.

President Kennedy, when asked about this apparent violation of Alliance for Progress commitments, replied that the United States did not have a consistent policy regarding military coups because "the circumstances sometimes are inconsistent."[12] The long and short of U.S. policy was that Washington preferred authoritarian regimes it could control over democratically elected governments with nationalist policies.

Another attempt at civilian rule occurred in 1966, but by this time the military was firmly entrenched. Juan Cesar Mendez Montenegro was elected president that year, but he entered office with his hands tied. He had signed a 16-point agreement with the military that severely limited his power. Although Mendez Montenegro favored negotiations with the guerrillas, the military refused to curb its counterinsurgency terror. During the next two years, 6-8,000 civilians were killed either by the army or the newly formed death squads like La Mano Blanca (The White Hand). During Mendez Montenegro's term in office, military assistance by U.S. advisers increased as did AID's involvement in pacification efforts. In 1970, the military resumed direct control of the presidency, holding it until 1986 when the military high command permitted another civilian, Vinicio Cerezo, to take office.

Gordon L. Bowen in his 1984 study in Armed Forces and Society called the U.S. economic and political intervention in the post-1954 period a case of "penetration politics." Caught up in cold war paranoia and its allegiance to U.S. corporate interests, the U.S. government changed the balance of Guatemalan political forces. Rather than pushing for a return to civilian rule, the United States stressed "the expansion of the military's role in Guatemalan social and political life."[13] In the 1960s, U.S. counterinsurgency assistance and military civic action programs broadened the mission of the military to include both the internal security and the development of Guatemala.

PACIFYING WITH AID AND COUNTER-TERROR

While reformers vainly tried to loosen the military's stranglehold through elections, several guerrilla groups formed in the 1960s to challenge military rule. On November 13, 1960, a group of young officers led by Alejandro de Leon, Marco Antonio Yon Sosa, and Luis

Turcios Lima led an internal rebellion against the military high command. They were angered by deepening military corruption and preparations underway by the United States to mount an invasion of Cuba from Guatemala soil. Loyal troops crushed the rebellion but Yon Sosa and Turcios Lima survived and went on to form the first guerrilla army, named the Alejandro de Leon November 13 Movement (MR-13) after their fallen comrade-in-arms.

Ironically, it was the jungle-warfare training the rebel officers had received at the U.S. counterinsurgency school at Fort Gulick in the Panama Canal Zone that gave them the expertise they needed to fight a guerrilla war. The MR-13 was quickly joined by a guerrilla front opened by the Guatemalan Communist Party, and in late 1962 a broad guerrilla army called the Rebel Armed Forces (FAR) established bases in the northeastern provinces of Zacapa and Izabal.

Shortly after the thwarted rebellion of 1960, the Pentagon sent a Civil Affairs Mobil Military Training Team (CAMTT) to Guatemala. The task of this team was to introduce the Guatemalan military to the concept of military/civic action programs and to establish a civil affairs division within the army structure. It was hoped that civic action projects would improve the public image of the military especially in rural areas through health and education programs, road-building and other public works projects. The Pentagon called these efforts nation building or civic action. While the stated objective of these programs was to improve military-civilian relations, the result was to give the military a place in the planning and implementation of national development.[14]

Guatemala was the Pentagon's first experiment with military civic action in Latin America. In his book Counterinsurgency Warfare, Major John Pustay wrote that the CAMTT "conducted civic action training programs in fourteen Army commands, indoctrinating four hundred officers in the process, and prepared a comprehensive plan for nation-building operations."[15] The new Guatemalan civil affairs division adopted the slogan "Accion Civica Militar--Seguridad y Progreso." Emblems worn by soldiers in Guatemala still bear the "Security and Progress" catchphrase of civic action. With U.S. help, the Guate-malan army formed the country's first Boy Scout troops and sponsored the annual Army Day.[16]

As guerrilla operations increased in the 1960s, U.S. involvement in the country's civic action and counterinsurgency programs also expanded. More U.S. advisers arrived, and in 1963 AID created its own civic action office to coordinate its own development programs with the military/civic action efforts underway in areas of guerrilla activity. Appointed to direct this office was the former head of the U.S. Southern Command's (SOUTHCOM) civic action division.

Under U.S. guidance, the Guatemalan Army established its Pilot Plan to confront the deepening insurgency. This called for the military to 1) improve relations with the civilian population, 2) function better as an instrument of counterinsurgency, and 3) mobilize popular participation in anti-guerrilla activities.[17] The Pilot Plan's follow-up campaign incorporated what have become the standard elements of U.S.-designed counterinsurgency efforts: civic action programs, aerial bombing to reduce popular support in guerrilla strongholds, psychological operations, U.S. development assistance, and paramilitary counterterrorism. The United States remained deeply involved in every aspect of the counterinsurgency campaign (including the aerial bombing of suspected guerrilla positions) until the end of the decade when the remnants of the guerrilla leadership fled to Mexico.

When asked by Congress to explain the presence of the large number of U.S. advisers in Guatemala, Pentagon officials said that its soldiers were not involved in combat but were overseeing malaria eradication, health clinic construction, well drilling, and free lunch programs.18 A later report in Armed Forces and Society magazine also described the civic action functions of U.S. advisers:

> A conspicuous part of the counterinsurgency effort in Guatemala was the civic action and public relations project that was heavily funded by the U.S. Military Assistance Program.... While prevailing social and economic problems remained, an increasingly large segment of the rural population, especially in the Northeast, came to view the government, particularly the military, as a source of goods and services.19

AID worked hand-in-hand with the military/civic action programs in the conflict zones. Deane Hinton became director of the AID Mission in Guatemala in 1967 and played a key role in coordinating AID programs with the counterinsurgency campaign. Hinton had previously been involved in the pacification program in Vietnam and came to Guatemala directly from a position with the National War College in Washington.20

In 1967, Lincoln Gordon, the U.S. Coordinator for the Alliance for Progress, told Congress that AID was requesting more money for Guatemala because "the government's anti-guerrilla campaign has included stepped-up social and economic measures in the guerrilla zone." "Guerrilla activity," he explained, "tends to generate a need for increased U.S. development assistance."21 In line with the Pilot Plan's goals, AID projects in Zacapa and Izabal were meant "to calm the people down" by instituting economic development projects that would reduce popular support for the guerrillas.22 One Guatemalan campesino, commenting on pacification programs, told Eduardo Galeano, author of Guatemala: Occupied Country that "for us to get drinking water, it seems necessary to have guerrillas nearby."[23]

While AID and civic action teams were trying to win hearts and minds, counterinsurgency battalions were involved in a bloody campaign to eliminate the several hundred guerrillas. By the end of the decade, 20,000 or more Guatemalans were killed by counterinsurgency operations. U.S. advisers were doing more than instructing the Guatemalan Army, they were leading forays into the mountains and conducting intelligence and bombing missions. At a time when flag-draped coffins were coming back from Vietnam by the hundreds, the deaths of a couple dozen U.S. soldiers in Guatemala went virtually unnoticed in the United States. In 1968, SOUTHCOM sponsored a joint military operation with the Nicaraguan and Guatemalan armed forces in Izabal. The "training exercises" were appropriately called "Operation Hawk."

The formation of groups of "civilian collaborators" or "voluntary military commissioners" fulfilled the third objective of Guatemala's pilot counterinsurgency plan: the mobilization of popular participation in anti-guerrilla activities. At the height of the campaign (1966-68), U.S. advisers helped establish a network of paramilitary units, later known as death squads, to wage a campaign of counterterror against suspected leftists throughout the country. Most of the civilian deaths during this period have been attributed by human rights groups to these death squads.[24] Justifying the wave of terror, Colonel John Webber, the U.S. military attache in Guatemala, said: "That's the way the country is. The Communists are using everything they have, including terror. And it must be met." Webber acknowledged that "it was my idea and at my instigation that the technique of counter-terror had been implemented by the Guatemalan Army in the Izabal areas."[25]

This combination of civic action programs, terrorism, and repression managed to end the guerrilla rebellion by 1970. Colonel Carlos Arana Osorio, who served as chief Guatemalan officer in charge of the counterinsurgency campaign in the northeast, estimated that 70 percent of his success in pacifying Zacapa was due to the social work of the army and only 30 percent was due to the power of weapons.[26] Arana, however, is remembered for the latter. An estimated 20,000 civilians died during this decade-long campaign, and Arana's massacres earned him the "Butcher of Zacapa" epithet.

Just as its involvement in Guatemala in the 1950s had given the United States its first experience in stabilization in Latin America, its support of Guatemala's military regime in the 1960s gave the United States its first taste of pacification and counterinsurgency in the region. For the Guatemalan military, the counterinsurgency war of the 1960s and almost two decades of U.S. military training prepared it for the next outbreak of insurgency. To pacify communities linked to the rebels, the army in the 1980s is again using civic action programs, international economic aid, and psychological operations. The scope and role of current pacification programs, however, go far beyond previous levels.

Indian Rebellion and Counterinsurgency

The terror unleashed by the army and the right-wing death squads succeeded in keeping the country relatively free of organized popular resistance until the mid 1970s, when peasant leagues, labor unions, Christian associations, and students formed to protect their interests and demand reforms. Since 1971, two new guerrilla groups--Guerrilla Army of the Poor (EGP) and Organization of People in Arms (ORPA)--had been patiently and quietly organizing the populations of the northwestern and western provinces. In sharp contrast to the earlier guerrilla armies, EGP and ORPA worked closely with the country's Indian communities and counted many Indians among their leaders. The first military action of the new guerrilla movement occurred in 1975 when the EGP assassinated a hated plantation owner in the Ixcan area of Quiche province.

The upsurge in popular organizing and the new outbreak of insurgency were met with a new wave of terror. This time the focus of the military violence was the Indian-populated provinces in western Guatemala--a region known as the Altiplano or highlands. In the late 1970s, the military targeted the provinces of Quiche, Huehuetenango, Alta Verapaz, Baja Verapaz, and Chimaltenango, which were the provinces where popular organizing and support for the guerrillas was most widespread. Currently, the counterinsurgency war has extended to most of western and southwestern Guatemala and to the northern province of Peten.

From 1978 to 1982, President Romeo Lucas Garcia and his brother Defense Minister Benedicto Lucas Garcia directed the counterinsurgency campaign. The military aimed to crush all signs of resistance in the highlands--from church groups concerned with social justice to peasant unions. While the war was ostensibly against the guerrillas, the actual targets of military violence were Indian communities suspected of sympathizing with the guerrilla cause. By burning villages and terrorizing Indians, the army hoped to weaken the guerrillas by severing all links between them and rural communities which they depended on for supplies and information.

During the four years of the Lucas Garcia government, the highlands region was put under military siege and death squad activity was rampant throughout the country. General Efrain Rios Montt took power in a March 1982 coup d'etat. He promised to end the corruption and repression that characterized the Lucas Garcia regime, and thereby also improve the country's international reputation. While death-squad violence in the cities markedly declined, Rios Montt continued the counterinsurgency campaign with a new vengeance. Trained at U.S. counterinsurgency schools and a former director of the Inter-American Defense College in Washington, Rios Montt was well prepared to oversee the military's offensive against the guerrilla rebellion. Rios Montt relied on his defense minister, General Oscar Mejia Victores, to oversee counterinsurgency operations. Rios Montt and Mejia Victores continued the scorched earth tactics of the Lucas brothers but also stressed the need for economic aid and civic action programs to counter the guerrillas.

The country's military elite had learned the importance of pacification programs that "win the hearts and minds" of rural communities in training courses of the Special Warfare School at Fort Bragg and in counterinsurgency seminars at Fort Davis in the Canal Zone. The officers were introduced to concepts like strategic hamlets, refugee resettlement programs, military civic action, and civil defense--many of which had been used during the Vietnam War. Beginning in the late 1970s, at the same time that U.S. aid dropped off because of a congressional ban on aiding gross violators of human rights, Guatemala received critical counterinsurgency training from Taiwan and Israel.

Army officers now study the techniques of counterinsurgency at Guatemala's own Center for Military Studies and Polytechnical Institute. The Army's military journal Revista Militar keeps officers informed about the latest developments in counterinsurgency theory, frequently running translations of articles published first in Military Review or other military magazines in the United States.

A PACIFICATION PLAN FOR THE 1980s

When Rios Montt and his advisers took over the counterinsurgency war in 1982, they decided that burning down Indian villages and murdering suspected supporters of the guerrillas was not enough to crush the Indian rebellion. While the "scorched earth" tactics of Lucas Garcia remained a part of the army's war on the highlands, the revised counterinsurgency strategy recognized the need for "development" as well as "security." The new approach was outlined in the National Plan of Security and Development, which was approved by the military regime a month after Rios Montt took over the National Palace.[1]

The National Plan of Security and Development stressed the need both to eliminate the "subversives" and to maintain better control over the population in the conflictive zones.[2] As part of its security planning, the Rios Montt government also called for the eventual return to civilian government as one of its long-term goals. It called for measures: "To restructure the electoral system....to re-establish the constitutional order of the country as a matter of urgency."[3]

The "security" half of the new counterinsurgency plan was optimistically labelled Victoria 82. The three main objectives of Victoria 82 were:

1. Deny the subversives access to the population who constitute their political and social base of support.

2. Rescue where possible individual members of the [guerrillas'] Irregular Local Forces, neutralizing or eliminating any who do not wish to be integrated into normal life.

3. Eliminate the enemy's Permanent Military Units.[4]

Rios Montt called the "development" half of his counterinsurgency plan "Beans and Guns" ("Frijoles y Fusiles). This pacification program introduced by Rios Montt in 1982 was also known as the Plan of Assistance to the Areas of Conflict (PAAC). The military, under the "Beans and Guns" pacification program, began organizing all the men and teenage boys in the conflict areas into civil defense patrols or PACs (Patrullas de Autodefensa Civil). Obligated to guard the entrances and patrol the streets of all highlands villages, the PACs were developed by the military not to defend Indian communities but to maintain close control over the Indian population.

Men and women received food allotments in exchange for labor performed on public works projects approved by the military. These food-for-work programs served to increase Indian dependency on the military while at the same time providing labor for its "development" projects. Colonel Pablo Mendoza, an officer stationed at the Huehuetenango military base, said that the "Beans and

Guns" strategy put the National Plan of Security and Development into action: "For so long, 20 years, we've been fighting the subversives and we have realized that only bullets, only guns, don't resolve the dilemma." According to Mendoza, the fundamental elements of the "Beans and Guns" approach to counterinsurgency were: "Restore the security of the population, win back those who are involved in the subversion, and kill those who are armed. That's it."[5]

CONDITIONS IN RURAL GUATEMALA

* Indians compose 46 percent of the total national population and 67 percent of the overall rural population.

* Non-Indians in Guatemala have a life expectancy of 58 but Indians can expect to live only 44 years.

* 80 percent of rural children are malnourished. The country has the worst income distribution in Central America.

* Unemployment is 50 percent in rural Guatemala.

* In the highlands, arable land per capita has declined precipitously from 2.5 acres in 1950 to 1.7 in 1964, 1.3 in 1973, and 1.2 in 1980.

* 54 percent of all Guatemalan farms have less than 4 acres but at least seven acres is needed for subsistence.

* Terms of trade for the small farmer have declined over 30 percent since 1975.

Sources: AID Mission, 1986 Country Strategy Statement; Centro de Consultoria (CESINSA) (Guatemala City, 1982).

Victoria 82 did not succeed in eliminating the EGP guerrillas but by 1983 the Army did regain control of most of the Altiplano and the Northern Transverse Strip (Franja Transversal del Norte.)* Army terror had made Indians think twice about supporting the guerrillas. And the "Beans and Guns" pacification strategy, while it might not have won the hearts and minds of the Indian communities, did increase military control over the highlands population. Together, the scorched earth tactics of the Army's elite troops and the pacification plan broke the strong and oftentimes open links that had been developing between the Indian population and the EGP guerrillas.

The U.S. Embassy recently assessed the pacification program of Rios Montt as a major step in restoring peace in the Guatemalan highlands. "As a result of increased attention by the army to the needs of the people of the Indian highlands," the U.S. Embassy stated, "the government made considerable headway against the insurgency both in the capital and in the main areas of conflict."[6]

Although pleased with the counterinsurgency campaign, the military high command in 1983 grew dissatisfied with Rios Montt. He angered the military high command by bypassing the traditional hierarchy in his decision making. His fanatical evangelicalism and his economic policies lost him support within the military. In August 1983, Rios Montt's defense minister, Oscar Humberto Mejia

---

* The Northern Transverse Strip is a vast swath of lowlands that transverses the northern reaches of the provinces of Alta Verapaz, Quiche, and Huehuetenango. The Ixcan or Playa Grande area was one of the early strongholds of the EGP guerrillas, and in 1976 was selected by AID as the site for its colonization project with the military government.

Victores, also a product of U.S. counterinsurgency training, led a military coup that named him the new chief-of-state. During the regime of General Mejia Victores (August 1983-January 1986), the military expanded the pacification campaign, giving increased attention to the non-military aspects of counterinsurgency.

Sign outside the military post in the Quiche province reads: "Only he who fights has the right to win. Only he who wins has the right to live."

SOLDIERS AS SOCIAL WORKERS

Soon after he seized control, General Mejia Victores announced measures to extend the pacification program begun by Rios Montt. Calling his new plan Firmeza 83, Mejia Victores set out to broaden military control over rural population in order to prevent another peasant rebellion. The main elements of the expanded pacification plan were refugee resettlement, rural development, psychological operations, model villages, and development poles.

The army's work plan for Firmeza 83 included the following directives:

* Areas of conflict should now be called areas of harmony ("areas de concordia").

* All forces of the public sector should be integrated into the campaign as well as religious and private institutions.

* In a conflict area, the military commander of the zone is the chief of all operations, civil and military.

* The orders of the military commander should be executed without comment by workers of government ministries. If not, they run the risk of being labeled subversive.[7]

As a way of institutionalizing Firmeza 83, Mejia Victores upgraded the old Civil Affairs Division formed in 1961. In 1983 he gave the new Section of Civil Affairs and Community Development (S-5) vast powers. The upgraded S-5 became a one of the five major military command sections with direct authority over 12 newly created Civil Affairs companies throughout rural Guatemala.[8] These Civil Affairs companies were put in charge of civil defense patrols, model villages, development poles, and psychological operations. While the S-5 have no "offensive capacity," they are responsible for "the organization of the community, its education, social promotion, health, sanitation, and local development."[9] The U.S. military's Civil Affairs section is also called S-5, but its S-5 functions only in foreign countries.[10]

The other military organization given new authority was the Committee for National Reconstruction (CRN), which had been established in 1976 to manage earthquake relief programs. The director of CRN and five of its ten directors are high military officers, but most of its workers are civilians. CRN's executive secretary Oscar Gallegos explained the institution's change of purpose: "Before we responded to a natural disaster, now we are responding to a human disaster."[11] Under Rios Montt, CRN had managed the collection and distribution of the food supplies for the "Beans and Guns" program. By late 1983, CRN was also playing a major role in the supervision of refugee resettlement, rural development, and job programs in the conflict zones. "Trabajo, Techo, y Tortillas" (Work, Shelter, and Food) became the new army slogan for pacification. While still controlled internally by the military, CRN's funding and operations are currently overseen by the Ministry of Urban and Rural Development, which was created immediately before Cerezo took office.

CRN determines the level of need in selected communities and manages the supply network for the military pacification efforts. It serves as the channel for all international aid to the conflict zones and has authority over the activities of all voluntary organizations in those areas. The CRN directorate has called its work "military humanism," and boasts that its relief and development activities have begun to rectify the socio-economic problems in the Guatemalan countryside. "These are no longer times," said CRN in 1985, "of impoverished committees, honorable ladies' charity associations, or groups of dreamers."[12] In Guatemala, charity and humanism have become a military mission.

OPERATION IXIL: TESTING GROUND FOR PACIFICATION

Even before Rios Montt seized control of the government, military strategists were mapping out a sophisticated pacification campaign. The first military planning for pacification focused on the Ixil Triangle—the part of northern Quiche where support for the guerrillas had been the strongest. Because of this support, the Ixil Triangle—demarcated by the three towns of Santa Maria Nebaj, San Juan Cotzal, and San Gaspar Chajul—had been the scene of some of the worst military massacres. The countryside is still scarred by 49 burnt and abandoned villages. A 1981 military document called Operation Ixil: Plan for Civil Affairs[13] set forth a range of pacification techniques for use in the Ixil Triangle. All subsequent pacification programs in Guatemala have been drawn from this document.

Operation Ixil proposed a two phase campaign. The first comprised the military measures required to "secure" the area. The goals of phase one included: "finishing off the subversives," "finishing the implementation of the ideological campaign," and "completing the organization of the civil defense patrols."

The second phase introduced pacification programs. The main goal was to return the Ixil Triangle "to law and order by convincing the local population to be more patriotic." According to the analysis presented in the Operation Ixil plan, the government had lost control of the Indian people because of their geographic and cultural isolation from national social and political life. Once military control was re-established, the plan said that programs should relate "more to the socioeconomic character of the region than to military or political issues."

Operation Ixil presented a multifaceted pacification plan designed to secure control of the population through education, development assistance, work programs, and

Watching over a refugee resettlement camp near the town of Rabinal in Baja Verapaz.

model villages for refugees and suspected guerrilla sympathizers. Operation Ixil included a "Campaign of Psychological Action," which was to be an "intense, profound, and well planned psychological campaign to capture the mentality of the Ixils in order to make them feel part of the Guatemalan nation."

While Operation Ixil stressed the importance of bilingual instruction, it also specified that "one half of the time in all education programs in the region should include instruction related to the ideological war and patriotic struggle." The educational goals of pacification could be achieved through weekly "re-education meetings" for the adults. In sum, Operation Ixil advocated measures to create "a new way of life" in the highlands, or better put, to further the process of the "ladinizacion" of the Ixil Indians.

Operation Ixil sketched out an organizational system that was later used as a model for the Inter-Institutional Coordination Committees (IICCs), which were instituted by Mejia Victores in late 1983. The IICCs formed a network used by the military to coordinate operations of all government ministries responsible for some aspect of rural development.

Operation Ixil proposed that all representatives of government agencies and ministries "be placed under military control until the termination of Operation Ixil, although their salaries and loans would continue to come from the institutions they serve." Pacification activities would be carried out in the following areas: Judicial Affairs; Public Health; Finance; Education; Work and Social Welfare; Agriculture; Economy, Commerce, and Industry; and Communications and Public Works. According to this proposal, a coordinating body for Ixil would include representatives from 13 different government agencies. Those agencies named in the plan were IGS, INTECAP, INAFOR, INTA, INDE, ICTA, INFOM, INGUAT, INDECA,

BANDESA, CORFINA, GUATEL, and INACOP--all of which have recently received funding from AID.

The success of the army's multidimensional pacification program in the Ixil Triangle resulted in the establishment of areas called development poles ("polos de desarrollo") in the different conflict zones. The Ixil Triangle and the Ixcan/Playa Grande area in the Northern Transverse Strip were designated by the military in 1984 as the first of the country's seven Development Poles. Each geographical pole was to become a center of economic, political, and social development.

In two years, pacification in Guatemala had evolved from the rudimentary "Beans and Guns" approach initiated by Rios Montt to a sophisticated strategy that integrated all the main elements of a textbook pacification campaign. Borrowing AID terminology, the military called this new, improved approach "integrated rural development."

A 1984 government decree (65-84) established the development poles of the highlands as the "maximum priority" for all public ministries.[14] Working under the supervision of the IIOCs and the CRN, the health ministry established health clinics in the model villages, the education department ran the schools, the electricity agency brought in power lines, the ministry of agriculture sent out agronomists, the housing agency contributed architects, and the public agricultural bank provided credit. All the agencies counted on international funds, particularly from AID and Inter-American Development Bank (IDB), for their work in the highlands.

THE ARMY AS DEVELOPMENT COORDINATOR

The main Guatemalan players in the expanded pacification plan under Mejia Victores were the army's Civil Affairs or S-5 section, CRN, and the Inter-Institutional

Coordination Committees (IICCs). A November 1984 decree, "The Organic Law of the National System of Inter-Institutional Coordination for Reconstruction and Development," established the current IIC system. It is a four-tiered network (national, provincial, municipal, and local) created:

> To orient and coordinate the actions and efforts of the public sector and of non-governmental organizations, together with popular participation, in the generation, execution, felicitation and operation of plans, programs, and projects aimed at achieving the reconstruction and development of the country at the national, departmental, municipal, and village levels.[15]

Designed by the army, the IICCs allowed the army to exercise control over all governmental and non-governmental development work in the conflict areas. The chief of staff for national defense was designated as the presiding officer of the national coordinating council. Also included in the national council were the S-5 chief, the secretary general of the National Office of Economic Planning (SEGEPLAN), the CRN director, the government's budget director, and the manager of the national Institute for Public Administration. Military zone commanders served as presidents of the provincial IICCs. The IICCs at the municipal and village level included the local mayors, but the commander of the local military maintained veto power over all committee decisions.

Many national and international observers describe the IICCs as a legal way to extend the military's power and give the military de facto control over rural Guatemala. The Guerrilla Army of the Poor (EGP) has stated that the essential purpose of the IICC system is "the establishment and the reinforcement of military control."[16]

In an attempt to reduce military control over the IICCs, President Vinicio Cerezo changed the composition and structure of the coordination councils. The national IICC was placed under the Ministry of Rural and Urban Development (a new ministry created in the final days of the Mejia Victores government) and the newly appointed provincial governors became the presidents of the IICC in each of the country's 22 provinces. At each level, however, military officers remain part of the IICCs and will likely continue to control their operations.

DEVELOPMENT POLES: A VISION OF PACIFICATION

Each of the seven development poles (See Map) cover a predominantly Indian-populated area where support for the guerrillas has been the strongest and the violence most intense. Over 440 razed Indian villages lie within these development poles.[17]

While the entire area theoretically benefits from the army's development initiatives, the attention is centered on the model villages constructed within the poles. These model villages are resettlement camps for Indians displaced by counterinsurgency violence. They are similar to the strategic hamlets used for pacification purposes by the United States and the South Vietnamese Army during the Vietnam War. With the help of civil defense patrols, the army has rounded up many of these refugees, most of whom were severely malnourished and disease ridden. Once under military control, the refugees are often obligated to build the model villages and to reconstruct other infrastructure, including roads, schools and bridges destroyed during the height of the violence. For their work, the Indians receive food provisions supplied by the United Nations and the United States but distributed by the army, government agencies, and PVOs.

Most of the model villages under army supervision are located on the very sites of Indian settlements destroyed by the army only a few years before. By early 1986, approximately 50,000 Indians were living in the so-called model villages. Construction is either underway or completed on 24 of the 50 or more model villages planned by the army. The government's National Housing Bank (BANVI) called the model villages "a new concept for human settlement of rural areas" that were "based on experience with security and control centers while providing services for the population."

The army says that the great advantage of living in these model villages is that residents receive the protection of a military outpost located on the edge of the village and enjoy the benefits of development projects.

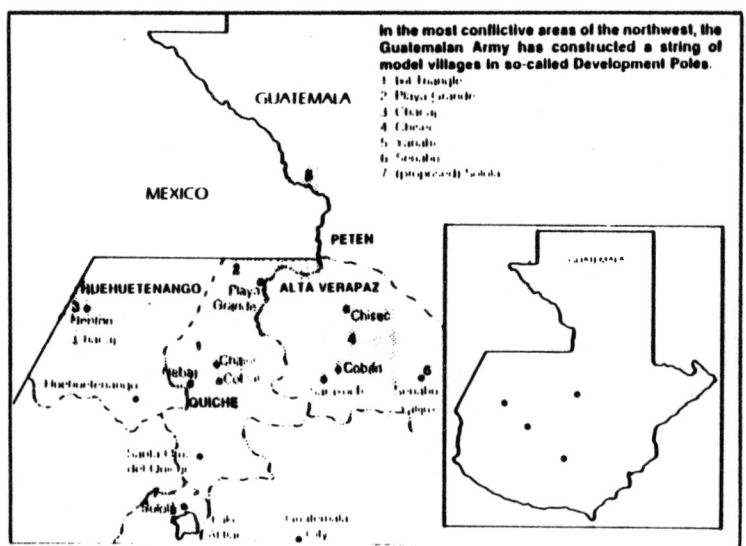

The army calls them "small paradises," but the militarized nature of these new villages prompted the Archbishop of Guatemala City to call them "anti-model villages."[18]

LIVING ON LIBERTY STREET

Located in the center of the Ixil Triangle is the model village of Acul, the first model village completed by the army. Displayed prominently in many village plazas throughout Quiche are S-5 posters exalting the accomplishments of Acul. The posters declare that Acul, the site of so much destruction "by the forces of subversion" has been healing the wounds of the past and allowing the "seeds of faith to open again in Guatemala." The poster boasts that, "While others talk and proselytize with demagoguery and the thunder of machine guns, the government preaches with its example."

Acul lies over the mountain from Nebaj, the major commercial center of the Ixil Triangle. The military finished an all-weather road to Acul in 1984, but only the military and government employees use the road. The Ixil Indians climb the mountain over the old dirt path. From the mountain top, you can see the many homes in the valley and on the mountain slopes that have been destroyed by the army. In Acul, the Indians live in two-room wooden houses laid out in a grid, each house with its own number on streets with names like "Liberty" and "Army." The new town stands in marked contrast to the former pattern of randomly placed homes dotting the countryside.

In the neighboring highlands province of Alta Verapaz, about 800 Kekchi and Poconchi Indians live in the model village of Acamal located within the Chisec development pole. The village is managed by Sergeant Julio Corsantes of S-5. Formerly a teacher, Corsantes joined S-5 in 1981, seldom wears a uniform, and regards himself more a social worker than a soldier.

Armed civil guards block the entrance to Acamal, and an army battalion is stationed ominously on a hilltop that overlooks the village. Inside the community center at Acamal is an architect's plastic design of what the village may one day become. The model resembles a North American suburb, complete with neat miniature churches, schools, cars in the streets, and rows of private homes surrounded by grass. What differentiates it from the normal suburban life is the placement of a helicopter and landing pad on the edge of the plastic village.

Covering the walls of the main room of the Acamal community center is a long registry of all the adult residents of the new village. The CRN director pointed out that Acamal residents had come from 22 different Indian villages, many of which no longer exist because of the "situation." Also listed in the registry are the different noms de guerre that Corsantes said were given by the guerrillas to their supporters. This and other information about the model village residents comes from interrogation sessions with S-5 officials. Pinned on the wall of the Acamal community center was a snapshot of Todd Sloan, AID's staff person for displaced persons, conferring with S-5 and CRN members at Acamal.

Cardboard signs posted in Acamal relay the message that the "communist subversives" deceived the Indians and led them on the path of violence:

> "Friend, why did you let the enemies of the country deceive you?"
>
> "Violence will be defeated by peace and progress."

Corsantes said that the residents at Acamal had recognized their mistakes and repented. "We are all working together now," he added with a public relations smile.[19]

The model village at Playa Grande, located in the Franja Transversal, is built at the center of an AID-funded (map B) colonization settlement that began in the late 1970s. The outbreak of war disrupted the AID project, and most of the settlers in this isolated region fled into the bush to escape the violence. Colonel Isaacs Rodriguez holds the guerrillas responsible for the many civilian deaths at the Playa Grande settlement. In contrast to refugee accounts of the wave of army terror, Rodriguez said that "the guerrillas burnt everything: houses, churches, health centers, everything." He said that the army's presence, with a military base that borders the new model village, was "to create a sense of security so the people would come back to their homes. We give the people security, and we give them food."[20]

In Playa Grande, the army works with CARE and AID in what Rodriguez calls a "community development program" in which the Indians build homes, schools, and other community infrastructure as well as cultivating the agro-export crop cardamom in return for a daily food allowance. In the overall development scheme for Playa Grande, Rodriguez said "the first step, the most important step is to build roads to these communities. Then 'techo minimo' (simple housing), electricity, and water."

As in the other model villages, psychological operations are a prominent part of the army's pacification efforts at Playa Grande. Explaining the need for the army's re-education program, Colonel Rodriguez said:

> When people return to their communities, they need ideological orientation to make them more responsible and to have a more patriotic, nationalist consciousness. This will make them more resistant to the subversion. At the model village of Playa Grande we have a meeting each week where they can talk about their problems. We call this re-education and development process the pacification plan of the country."

In the model villages, school children learn "respect for the flag, respect for the authorities, and how not to be deceived by the communist delinquents." After school is over for the day, the male Indian students, ages six through 14, regularly march through the dirt streets chanting:

> For Guatemala,
> We swear to fight,
> Against the subversion.
> Death to the subversives.
> Death to the communists.

DEVELOPMENT UNDER MILITARY SIEGE

Although the army did not eliminate the insurgents, it did succeed in isolating them. Massacres and village burnings struck fear into Indian communities, causing them to think twice about supporting the guerrillas. The wave of violence that swept through the highlands increased Indian hatred of the army but also resulted in widespread disillusionment with the rebel opposition. While the guerrillas demonstrated their ability to strike out at army targets, they did not prove capable of protecting their popular base of support. Those Indian families that joined the guerrillas commonly found that the rebel armies could guarantee them neither food nor shelter.

Before 1979, the army had divided the country into nine military zones with a large military base in each zone. In the course of the counterinsurgency war, the military high command has made each of the 22 Guatemalan provinces into a military zone, every one with its own army base. The militarization of rural Guatemala has also given rise to an extensive network of small army outposts located within most of the municipios (townships) caught up in the conflict. Besides their role in keeping their areas "secure," the commanders of these new bases and outposts also direct the army's "development" programs. Military control is especially strong in the huge Peten province which is managed by FYDEP, the military-tied government development agency for the province.

The Civil Patrols play a vital role in the militarization of rural Guatemala. Since 1982, PACs have become a central part of life in most Indian villages. By 1985, over 900,000 boys and men, mostly Indian, were serving without compensation in the civil patrol network. Although the PACs are nominally volunteer organizations, the army coerces Indian men and boys to serve by threatening to label them as subversives if they do not volunteer. The military high command has commended the PACs for having "doubled the efficiency of the security forces in creating the conditions of peace basic to the integrated development of these communities, especially those which are most remote from urban areas."[21] Immediately before leaving office, Mejia Victores passed a decree which legalized the PACs, renamed them Civil Defense Committees, and defined them as "civil" organizations to be assisted and coordinated by the Ministry of Defense.[22]

Also before turning power over to the new civilian president, the outgoing regime approved several other decrees aimed at institutionalizing its security and development programs. One decree called the results of the Plan of Assistance to Conflict Areas "extremely encouraging" and effective in "reducing the general causes of violence." The decree, which was interpreted as an authorization for the continuation of PAAC, requisitioned several million pounds of basic grains from the government's reserves for use by the Ministry of Defense. In his final days, Mejia Victores also mandated the creation of a new State Security Council. Similar to the U.S. National Security Council, the new institution will bring together defense, intelligence, and civilian ministries. The decisions of this permanent council will be carried out by the newly created Secretary of Intelligence and National Security. And to add an extra measure of security, Mejia Victores announced a "general amnesty" for every person responsible or accused of having committed political crimes and related common crimes since 1982.

Soldiers guard resettlement camp in the mountains of Baja Verapaz near the town of Rabinal.

FOUR YEARS OF PACIFICATION

Victoria 82 (Victory): Introduction by Rios Montt of the building blocks of pacification: food-for-work programs, reorganized and expanded civil defense patrols, and refugee resettlement by the army. The programs, known as "Beans and Guns," took place alongside a campaign to terrorize Altiplano Indians.

Firmeza 83 (Strength): Under Mejia Victores, the pacification programs introduced under **Victoria 82** were extended. Development poles and model villages were initiated, and the military strengthened its control over all government ministries through its new Civil Affairs Section and the incipient Inter-Institutional Coordination Committees.

Reencuentro Institucional 84 (Institutional Renewal): The military government called for elections for the National Constituent Assembly, proclaimed a "democratic opening" to secure international aid, and intensified rural development in areas of conflict. The concept of development poles was broadened, and the Inter-Institutional Coordination Committees were extended to the department, municipal, and local levels.

Estabilidad 85 (Stabilization): Presidential elections were initiated, better international relations became a priority, pacification programs were further extended.

Pacification: A Joint Effort

The pacification campaign in Guatemala could not have pressed forward without international development funds and food donations. While the army oversees the campaign, it depends on foreign aid to implement its programs. The chief international participants in the country's pacification campaign are the following: 1) U.S. government through AID and Food for Peace (PL480) programs, 2) United Nations through its World Food Program (WFP), 3) PVOs (private voluntary organizations); and 4) Israel and Taiwan, countries which have provided training, technical assistance, and arms.

Since 1954 AID has been a major figure in Guatemala. Almost every Guatemalan ministry has received AID funds; the rural roads department, the planning department, and the agricultural extension service actually owe their existence to AID. During the Carter Administration, new AID funds for the government of Guatemala were cut off as a result of U.S. displeasure with the country's continuing violation of human rights. Although new funds to the government were blocked, AID funds continued to flow into Guatemala through previously authorized assistance packages and through the programs of PVOs.

Human rights violations have not stopped President Reagan from advocating increased aid for Guatemala. Since the beginning of his first term, President Reagan has pushed Congress to approve escalating sums of economic and military aid for Guatemala. Economic aid from the United States has been steadily rising since 1980,

U. S. MILITARY AND ECONOMIC AID TO GUATEMALA, 1949-1987
($ million)

	1949-1979	1980-1983	1984	1985	1986* estimate	1987* requested
IMET	7.5	0.0	0.0	0.5	0.3	0.5
MAP	16.4	0.0	0.0	0.0	4.8	10.0
FMS	10.9	0.0	0.0	0.0	0.0	0.0
Total Military	34.8	0.0	0.0	0.5	5.1	10.5
DA	256.0	37.4	4.5	58.5	33.0	40.0
PL480 Title I	0.0	0.0	6.7	21.0	14.0	19.0
PL480 Title II	59.2	21.8	6.5	4.4	4.4	4.7
ESF	33.7	10.0	0.0	12.5	47.9	70.0
Total Economic	348.9	69.2	17.7	96.4	99.3	133.7
TOTAL	383.7	69.2	17.7	96.9	104.4	144.2

IMET = International Military Training, MAP = Military Assistance Program, FMS = Foreign Military Sales, DA = Development Assistance, ESF = Economic Support Funds, PL480 = U.S. Food Assistance.
* 1986 and 1987 figures will probably increase through supplemental appropriations.

Source: AID, U.S. Overseas Loan and Grants, July 1, 1945-September 30, 1984; James Cason, Guatemala Desk Officer State Department, February, 1986.

jumping from $11 million in 1980 to $97 million in 1985. In 1986, aid rose to $104 million with $144 million scheduled for 1987.

And virtually all U.S. economic aid has been targeted for the highlands. The U.S. emphasis on the highlands parallels the Guatemalan military's own attention to that region. The Guatemalan presidential elections of late 1985 paved the way for greatly increased foreign aid--a large percentage of which will be channeled through institutions with strong ties to the military.

AID has kept in the shadows of pacification in Guatemala. From 1982 to 1985, AID vigorously denied that any of its funds were going into the model villages or the development poles even though it was channeling counterpart funds and PVO grants into those areas. Rather than directly funding the CRN and the military's pacification program, AID specified that local currency created from Economic Support Funds (ESF) and Title I food sales (see below) be used for the military government's rural development programs in the highlands.

On several occasions during this period of the formation of the development poles, AID specified that its funds go directly to model villages in Huehuetenango and Alta Verapaz. By 1985 AID publicly acknowledged that its programs might have been used within the development poles and actually proposed a program to fund the local IICCs within the development poles. In a March 6, 1985 letter to Senator Patrick Leahy, AID's Jay F. Morris said:

> Our programs have been conceived, designed, and executed independently, and there has been no plan or attempt to coordinate these programs with the model villages program. Since our regular programs operate all over the

> western highlands, however, it is conceivable that some activity in agriculture, health, education, or family planning may have provided services in an area designated as a Pole of Development or model village area....The formerly displaced persons who settle in the model villages, however, have at least the same degree of need as other low-income persons in the highlands, and so in the future, we would not seek to exclude them from services and benefits provided by civilian ministry programs of broad region-wide scope which we support.[1]

While AID may not have assisted in the planning of the pacification campaign, as it did in the 1960s and as it is currently doing in El Salvador, AID assistance has provided many of the building blocks on which that campaign is based. Without U.S. economic assistance, the military could never have mounted such an extensive pacification campaign.

Grants and loans from AID have not gone directly to the military's Civil Affairs Section. Instead, AID has channeled its economic assistance through military-controlled organizations like the CRN and through the Inter-Institutional Coordination Councils. "The predominant thinking in Guatemala," said Gary Adams, AID's desk officer to Guatemala, "is that you can get more done with honey than with bullets. You provide people with honey and that takes them away from the guerrillas."[2] And it is AID that is the main supplier of "honey" to the Guatemalan government.

The United States has acknowledged the connection between Guatemala's development programs and its counterinsurgency campaign. The U.S. Embassy noted in 1983 that the "food, shelter, and work" programs of the Guatemalan government were initiated as part of a "counterinsurgency social-action program."[3] But both the AID Mission and the U.S. Embassy in Guatemala have denied any joint planning of or significant assistance for pacification programs in the highlands. The almost one-to-one correspondence between AID's rural development programs in the highlands and the government's own development plan makes this denial less than credible.

In its 1984 budget request, AID noted that its development program coincided with that of the Guatemalan government. The AID Mission told Congress that it believed it important "to improve the current economic situation and address the political unrest in the Altiplano." AID said that it could implement all of its goals and at the same time "support the government of Guatemala's commitment to provide for the previously disadvantaged population in the Altiplano."

According to AID: "The government views AID as the best source of assistance in the development of the Altiplano, and consequently AID can have a major impact in shaping programs undertaken there."[4] Supporting the request for additional aid to Guatemala, AID Administrator Peter McPherson said that the program of the AID Mission in Guatemala "is directed at the rural poor, especially the Indians" and "addresses the underlying social/economic conditions which fan insurgency."[5]

Since 1983 the highlands and the Franja Transversal has become what AID calls its "target area" in Guatemala. AID directed its aid to the very parts of Guatemala designated as unsafe by a recent State Department Travel Advisory. By mid-1984, 80-90 percent of all AID funds were going to the very regions where army violence was most severe. According to AID in Washington, the focus on this part of the country had nothing to do with the Guatemalan government's own programs in the region but reflected AID's concern for the welfare of the resident Indian population.[6]

Justifying the fact that nine out of every ten AID projects in Guatemala involve the Altiplano population, Robert Queener, AID regional officer for Central America, stated:

> The highlands became more of a single-minded focus in the 80s because the people there have been left out. The Indians haven't received the benefits of development. Getting the government of Guatemala to develop the highlands is a policy change. The aid also helps social and political stability. We want to see that the government meets the needs of the Indians.[7]

SUPPLYING THE HONEY

The AID Mission in Guatemala supports the military's pacification programs in the following ways:

* Assistance goes to military-tied organizations like the Committee for National Reconstruction (CRN) through U.S. channels like Economic Support Fund (ESF) and Title I food agreements.

* Recent AID funds have gone to virtually all the government ministries working in the target areas.

* AID's disaster relief and PVO programs have assisted areas affected by "civil strife" including model villages and development poles.

* A large percentage of AID funds pay for rural roads in the conflict zones which are used predominantly by the military. PL480 food "pays" for forced labor for this road construction and other infrastructure projects.

* U.S.-supported food-for-work projects and programs to promote non-traditional exports are also the focus of the development component of the military's pacification campaign.

* Occasional AID relief funds and "techo minimo" construction materials have been sent to model villages.

CRN director Colonel German Grotewald said in 1984 that his organization "depends on AID for our programs in the highlands."[8] His executive secretary, Oscar Gallegos, boasted that CRN "doesn't spend a penny of its own fnds" for the development programs and services it oversees in the development poles.[9] The International Cooperation Division (ACNI) of CRN manages the foreign grants and the work of international PVOs. But as CRN makes explicit in its principles, the "programs and geographic destination of such international cooperation will be decided by CRN"--not by the international donor.[10] The 1984 annual report of ACNI explained that a fund of 2 million quetzales (equivalent at that time to $2 million), set up by the Guatemalan government as part of an agreement with AID, financed most of its joint programs with PVOs that year.[11] A more recent CRN report shows that AID funding has backed operations in the development poles in northern Huehuetenango and in Alta Verapaz.[12]

Similarly, Colonel Mario Paiz Bolanos, director of the army's Civilian Affairs division, explained that the army spends very little of its own funding on the highlands development plan. Instead, it coordinates all the development aid that goes to the Altiplano. Because of its role as coordinator of development, the Civilian Affairs office can make certain that AID-funded schools, housing, roads, and schools are placed in locations that the army regards as most strategic.[13] Another S-5 official, Dr. Luis Sieckavizza, noted that even though the United States may publicly disassociate itself from the military's civic action program, "there are a lot of ways to do it under the table."[14]

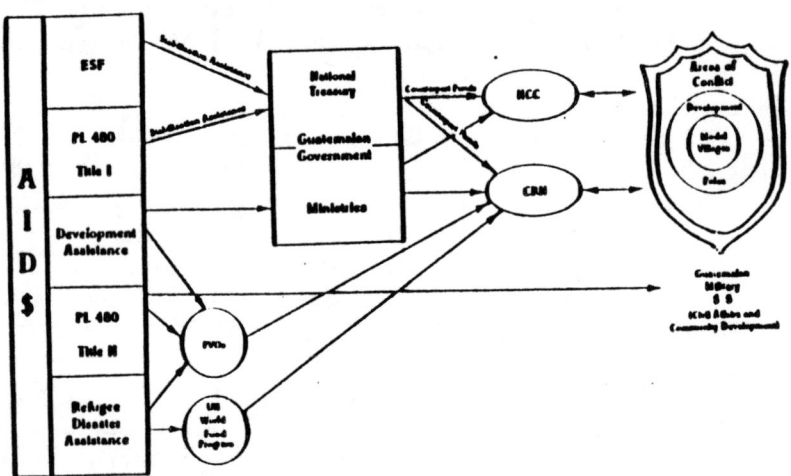

Siekavizza gave the example of a team of U.S. army doctors from U.S. military bases in Panama who were flown in to work in the model villages for 10 days.[15] He was referring to one of a series of SOUTHCOM's "tropical medicine training" programs that transports U.S. military doctors to rural spots in Central America. An article in the U.S. military journal Proceedings described such a training mission to the Ixil Triangle: "This little Indian girl and the Guatemalan adults with her are not likely to ever forget the dungaree-clad doctor from the U.S. Navy who helped her."[16]

As mentioned previously, all international relief and development projects in the highlands fall within the purview of the Inter-Institutional Coordination Committees. At the military post just outside the model village of Playa Grande, the area commander made it clear that the army controls the IICC. "I am the inter-institutional coordinator," said Colonel Isaacs Rodriguez. "All the public sectors are commanded by me." Rodriguez said that in Playa Grande the army was in charge of "community development" but depends on AID's economic aid projects like school construction, food distribution, and development projects.

Arthur Dewey, assistant secretary of the State Department's refugee program, told the Guatemalan army in late 1984 that he supported the return of refugees from Mexico to the model villages being constructed by the army along the border. Dewey also expressed support for the system of Inter-Institutional Coordination Committees. He called the resettlement work within Guatemala impressive. "My government looks favorably upon the poles of development," said Dewey, "because they show the goodwill of the government to grant Guatemalan refugees a better form of life since land, potable water, electricity, and other necessary services are being made available to them."17

AID has also applauded the military for its development poles program. In March 1985, it said that "the principal beneficiaries of the program are the inhabitants of the villages that are being rebuilt." The adverse economic situation of the Guatemalan government, however, limits the rapid implementation of the program. But AID says that the government "is encouraged by the rapid acceptance of this plan by the Highland Indians-- judging by their return to their lands and their provision of manual labor to rebuild their communities." And "the sooner these areas are reconstructed, the sooner the affected population can once again become productive members of society." Like CRN and the army, AID insists that Indians themselves are guiding the course of development in the highlands. According to AID, the "beneficiaries" of the model villages:

> ...help the CRN select the location and assist in the general design of their rebuilt town and its infrastructure. They also participate directly in the construction of their houses, water systems, roads, and other infrastructure. The strong desire to reestablish their lives has led these participants to work voluntarily under difficult physical conditions.[18]

PENTAGON SUPPORT FOR CIVIC ACTION

As early as 1982, the Pentagon tried to support the pacification campaign. A Pentagon official told Congress that the Guatemalan military desperately needed "engineering equipment for their civic action program" which was "tied to an insurgency program." During the budget hearings, Representative Stephen Solarz said that "to the extent the purpose of this program is to build roads, farm-to-market highways or other projects," then economic aid funds rather than military aid should be used for civic action.[19] Congress rejected this request, but a similar request for non-lethal military aid was approved for 1986. The Pentagon says this aid is scheduled to be used for non-armament spare parts and construction equipment and "for items of a humanitarian nature, such as medicine, civic action, medical evacuation helicopters and ambulances."[20]

The Guatemalan Army receives the highest compliments from the country's U.S. MilGroup. Defense Attache Colonel George Hooker, a veteran of Vietnam, said: "In my opinion, it's a pretty good little army. Despite lack of supplies, they have good morale and send out frequent combat patrols. The officers receive excellent training, and from Mejia (then president General Oscar Mejia Victores) on down they all have combat experience."

For Colonel David McGlaughlin, the commander of the country's MilGroup and also a Vietnam veteran, the development poles are "like our frontier towns in 1870." Asked about the barbed wire, "Sure, they need to keep the cows out of the corn." The U.S. MilGroup says that the army needs more U.S. aid for their civic action program, including more trucks, helicopters for medical evacuation, spare parts, bulldozers and graders for road construction, and a radial communication network.[21]

BACKING FROM MULTILATERALS

The Reagan Administration has also pushed the international financial institutions or multilateral banks to support Guatemala. In the last several years, the World Bank and the Inter-American Development Bank (IDB) have both initiated larger lending programs for Guatemala. Washington has also authorized loans for rural development in Guatemala through the Central American Bank of Economic Integration (CABEI).

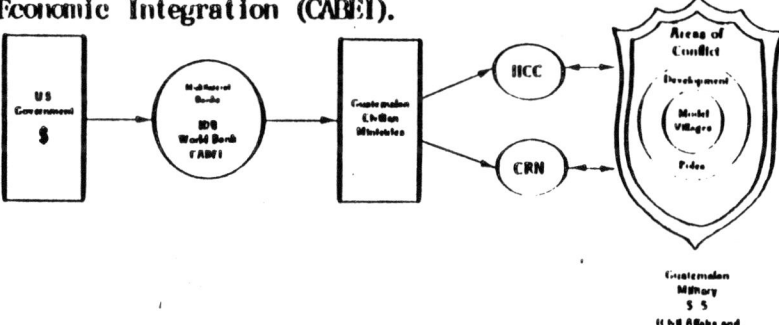

Because of its large financial commitments, the U.S. government can influence the lending decisions of these institutions, particularly IDB and CABEI. Since 1982, these multilaterals have funded a number of projects in coordination with AID and the military government including rural roads construction, the promotion of nontraditional agriculture, and rural communications. In 1985, these multilateral institutions had over $460 million of projects, mostly in rural development, in Guatemala.

FOOD FOR WORK AND CONTROL

From the outset of the "Beans and Guns" program of Rios Montt, food distribution by the army has been the foundation of pacification in Guatemala. Food donations come primarily from AID's PL480 program and the UN's World Food Program (WFP) but also from private groups like the Christian Broadcasting Network (CBN). The CBN has served as the coordinator of food distribution for the army.

The supplies for the food-for-work programs in the conflict areas are distributed by the WFP and U.S. PVOs (CARE and Catholic Relief Services). The source of most of this food is the U.S. PL480 program which AID administers.

The WFP distributes its food through the CBN, which uses the donations for food-for-work projects. These projects mostly involve road construction but also entail work on new housing, electrification, telegraph lines, schools, health centers, irrigation for vegetable production, and latrines in rural communities, mostly in conflict areas. A 1983 WFP agreement with CBN called for the construction of 1,200 kilometers of roads, 120 bridges, and 15,000 low-cost homes through food-for-work projects.[22] WFP's current food distribution program is valued at $50 million. In 1985, AID said that WFP's program "is closely coordinated with AID's plans to add new activities worth some $20 to $25 million." AID describes its relationship with WFP in Guatemala as "particularly close and fruitful."[23]

A WFP official in Guatemala readily acknowledged that its donations were being used by the military as part of its pacification and counterinsurgency plan in the Altiplano. "But you need to understand," he added, "that the United Nations judges its food aid not by politics but by need, and there's a lot of hunger in the highlands."24

The AID Mission in Guatemala City says that most of the food being distributed by the military in the model villages comes from the WFP not from the United States. Technically, this is true but virtually all WFP's supplies in Guatemala originally are provided to the United Nations by the United States. The familiar U.S. red-white-and-blue shield and the Alliance for Progress handshake are emblazoned across the bags of corn and cans of vegetable oil that the WFP hands out to the inhabitants of the development poles.

AID's food assistance flows through two PL480 programs: Title I and Title II. Title II covers the distribution of U.S. food to poor people through relief and food-for-work programs while Title 1 deliveries go directly to the host government as a way to assist the country financially.

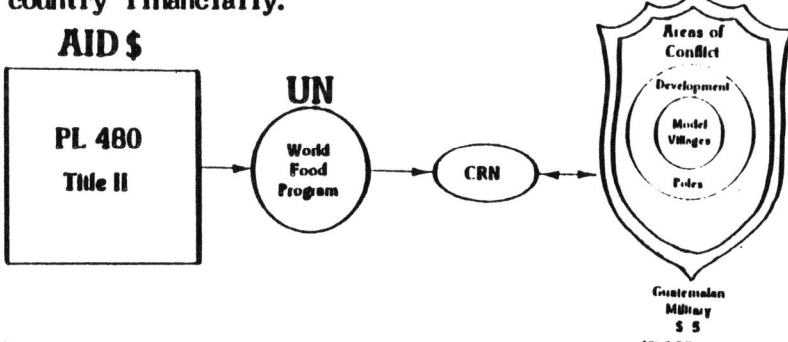

Unlike the WFP's program, PL480 food distribution programs (Title II) are administered by PVOs and are not directly channeled through the CRN. But like the WFP,

PL480 Title II food is distributed mostly in the highlands and largely through food-for-work and relief programs approved by the military. Although in many cases this food might not actually be distributed by CRN, the CRN and the Inter-Institutional Coordinating Councils coordinate all PL480 food distribution programs.

Its 1986 Country Development Strategy Statement recommended the expansion of the PL480 program "to provide for displaced persons who are temporarily located in safe-haven locations and to enhance the effectiveness of self-help labor in labor-intensive development programs in the target areas." The report noted that expanded food-for-work projects in the highlands could address the lack of services and infrastructure, which "has been identified as a major constraint to the development of the country, both politically and economically."

Explaining the logic of the food-for-work program, Saul Figueroa, the chief of the military's civilian affairs office in Huehuetenango, said, "If the subversives had invited these people to go with them and had given them a means of subsistence these people [the guerrillas] would be winning." Conversely, Figueroa would argue, the army is winning because it has the beans to hand out to hungry campesinos.[25]

Title I food differs from PL480 Title II food in that it goes directly to the recipient government which then sells the food on the internal commercial market. In Guatemala, as in other Central American nations, AID has used the Title I program to economically stabilize governments. The program is a boon to governments because it frees up foreign exchange (dollars) that would normally be spent importing food. Because the government sells this food, it provides an additional source of government revenue.

In 1984, for the first time in history, Guatemala received $7.5 million in Title I food. Title I support increased to $21 million in 1985 and is scheduled to remain at least that high for the rest of the decade. The 1984 Title I agreement required the Guatemala government to use the funds generated by the sales of Title I food aid for government-operated "community development projects" in the highlands. Along with ESF counterpart funds, the revenues generated by Title I sales cover a substantial part of CRN's budget. AID has said these funds are not being used in the model villages, but it also admits that it does not closely monitor local currency funds.26

Malnutrition and hunger are certainly serious problems in Guatemala, especially in the highlands. But the bags of corn and cans of vegetable oil bearing the U.S. emblem distributed to Indian men and women do not help resolve the long-term agrarian problems that are responsible for malnutrition and spark rural rebellion. In fact, it is the army's declared intention to use this international aid as an instrument of pacification and a way to avoid upheaval over issues like agrarian reform. The United Nations and the United States insist that the donated supplies are for humanitarian relief but they have not taken measures to see that the food comes free of political ties. A recent report by Americas Watch, a human rights monitoring group, concluded:

> International food aid becomes another instrument of military control. That is, hungry peasants must pledge allegiance to the government, work on government projects, and obey military commands in order to obtain food.... The situation provides the military with one more form of coercion, with one more weapon in its campaign to consolidate its control and domination of civilian life in the highlands."27

ROADS FOR BAREFOOT PEASANTS

For the last 30 years, road building has been a priority for economic aid programs in Guatemala. In the 1950s and 1960s, AID and its predecessor agency paid for the construction of the Atlantic and the Pacific highways. Washington announced that these were necessary infrastructure improvements to attract foreign investment and to promote the modern agro-export economy. An underlying assumption, however, was that revolutionary change would be less likely if the Guatemalan economy was yet more dependent on the international capitalist market.

By the late 1970s, the AID strategy had changed. Roads remained the number one priority, but the emphasis switched from coastal roads to rural access roads. AID said the extended transportation network in the Altiplano and the Franja Transversal would help initiate the production of agro-exports and integrate these areas into national political and economic life.

Since 1978 (the very year that the military unleashed its counterinsurgency terror in the highlands) about 40 percent of AID's development assistance budget has been used for rural roads in the highlands and the Franja Transversal. AID road construction funds have in the last several years been transferred to Caminos Rurales (the rural roads division of the transportation ministry), CRN, and the Institute for Agrarian Transportation (INTA). Before 1978 Caminos Rurales was a skeleton agency with virtually no budget. By 1984 the department had expanded from seven to over 300 employees with an annual budget of $8 million.

Road construction and maintenance programs are part of AID's agricultural development projects such as Small Farmer Development and the Highlands Agricultural Development. The other funders of rural road construction are the Inter-American Development Bank (IDB) and the Central

American Bank of Economic Integration (CABEI)--both of which depend on their funding from the United States. AID justifies its disproportionately large investment in rural roads on the grounds that the roads spark rural development by 1) increasing marketing opportunities for small farmers, particularly those growing non-traditional crops, 2) providing construction jobs for the unemployed, 3) facilitating the government's colonization and resettlement projects in frontier regions of the Franja Transversal, and 4) improving farmers' access to agricultural inputs like pesticides and fertilizer that are imported from the United States.

Among the positive effects of road building in the highlands, according to AID, is the increased integration of Indians into the dominant society and more contact with government representatives. This "should provide the incentive and the opportunity for Indians to learn Spanish, which in turn will assist Indian participation in the economic, social, and political mainstream."[28] In its Highlands Agricultural Development Project--in which more than half the budget is for road construction and maintenance--AID noted:

> Indians have traditionally isolated themselves and have been fearful of government and other official contacts. Their new appreciation of the government of Guatemala [resulting from increased contact] will have considerable significance in the development of a politically stable rural area."

In calling for better "integration" of highlands Indians into national life, AID echoes the sentiments of the Guatemalan military. But this view conveniently overlooks the integral although highly exploited role Indian laborers play in the national economy. The country's agroexport economy depends on the seasonal labor of highlands Indians, and the national economy also relies on Indian farmers to produce most of the country's basic grains. Indians, however, have been able to maintain a separate cultural identity and consider the nation's political system oppressive and contrary to their interests. AID and the country's military hope that a better transportation network in the highlands will break down this self-imposed isolation and thereby reduce the susceptibility of the Indian population to guerrilla organizing.

Like AID, the Guatemalan government has given rural roads in the highlands top priority. In 1985, the AID Mission observed: "At a time when other government ministries are being requested to reduce their budgets, the government is increasing its roads program."[29] This emphasis given to road building by the military government of Mejia Victores demonstrated "the government's commitment to provide access roads to needy farmers." The AID Mission makes no mention of the obvious military implications of improved rural transportation.

A review of the activity of Caminos Rurales and INTA shows that the overwhelming amount of new rural road construction has occurred in either the highlands or the Franja Transversal del Norte. Hundreds of kilometers of roads have been built in the development poles and lead to the model villages. Over half of the construction by Caminos Rurales since 1978 has occurred in Huehuetenago and Quiche--the two provinces most affected by the counterinsurgency war. Roads built by the government extend into the development poles of those two provinces.

Even though a counterinsurgency war was waging at the time, AID in 1984 said that labor-intensive roadbuilding is "an ideal type of project to implement within the current Guatemalan Highlands environment."[30] Not only will small farmers be able to market their surplus

Lining up for a food-for-work road construction project in the Nebaj plaza in the Ixil Triangle.

because of the roads, AID said, but the roadbuilding provides thousands of labor intensive jobs for the unemployed. For their "pick and shovel" work carving roads out along mountain slopes, Indian men are paid $1.00 a day or are compensated through food-for-work programs.

Since 1978 AID-sponsored projects have resulted in over 600 kilometers of road. Recently, AID has increased funds for new road construction. It has set in motion a project that will pay for the maintenance of 1300 kilometers of roads in the Altiplano. The latest rural roads program, called the Farm-to-Market Access Roads project, provides $10 million for the construction and rehabilitation of 800 kilometers of roads in the highlands. AID says the project "will provide more than 150,000 rural inhabitants with roads to market centers, providing incentives to produce higher value cash crops."31

AID continues to make rural roads projects its top development priority despite its failure to show that new or improved rural roads in the Altiplano have contributed significantly to the welfare of the area's Indian population. In fact, its only evaluation of the program showed little or no correlation between rural roads and the incomes of small farmers. The report noted that "farmers producing only for family consumption before roads were built did little better afterwards, since transport costs had not been their main production constraint." The evaluation pointed out that the farmers in one isolated Indian village "were not able to produce enough surplus for sale to benefit directly from the road." The report also stated that there had been no coordination between the placement of roads and the installation of other projects like irrigation systems that were supposed to help small farmers.[32]

The roads evaluation made no mention of the violent political situation in the highlands but the U.S.D.A. consultant who submitted the evaluation said privately: "The first thing these roads do is get the military out to where the action is," adding that "if the military wasn't up in these mountains there would be no violence."[33]

Most observers share the same opinion. A Guatemalan agronomist working on an AID small farmer project in San Marcos said, "You'll see right away that there is always a military outpost at the end of all the roads in the Altiplano. The roads are for the security of the country." Like most other Guatemalan government officials interviewed, he dismissed the argument that the roads were for the small farmers. "The Indians say, 'We don't need roads. We need other things but we don't need roads because we have our backs and we have our paths through the mountains.'"[34] Referring to new roads built in the Ixil Triangle, the army proudly declared that "the Indians no longer have to carry sacks of corn on their back over difficult paths."[35] Roads or not, Indians still walk. Many of them do not even own a pair of shoes let alone a truck to travel the new rural roads crisscrossing the highlands.

AID has insisted that all its development projects including road building benefit the highlands; it rejects all suggestions that its roadbuilding program is related to pacification in Guatemala. "If there is ever a tendency that the road will help anything other than the small farmer, we don't touch it," declared Lawrence Hill of the AID Mission in Guatemala.[36] Lawrence Ogle, another AID official, said that the placement of the roads is based on the agricultural potential of the area and on requests for new roads by community organizations.[37]

But interviews with officials from Caminos Rurales and INTA conflict with AID statements. In 1983, Minister of Communications Hugo Solares said that AID gave the military government funds to construct roads in the isolated areas of the northwestern highlands, including the sites of the new model villages. In 1984, Julio Galicia of Caminos Rurales said that virtually all rural road construction and maintenance in the highlands were backed by AID, including the roads that lead directly to the model villages and provided access to the development poles.[38] Decisions about the location of new road construction are made by AID and Guatemalan government officials, he said, not by the affected Indian communities.

David Lopez, the director of the rural roads department, said that AID has funded about half of all Caminos Rurales road construction. While he said that AID asked that its funds not go directly to the development poles, Lopez explained that AID funds are mixed in with all other department funds. Lopez said that AID funding in 1986 will allow the department to greatly expand its operations.[39]

Through its Small Farmer Development Project, AID has financed the construction of new roads into the Franja Transversal del Norte. The roads are part of an ongoing AID-funded project that settled 5000 families into this strategically-important zone. The civilian-military elite in Guatemala welcomed AID's initiatives in this northern strip not only as a way to establish a stronghold in this isolated border region but also as a help to making this rich agricultural area more accessible. Guatemalans commonly refer to the Franja Transversal region as the "Zone of Generals" because, as soon as new roads opened up the region, army officers appropriated the best land.

PVOs PITCH IN

Guatemala experienced its first wave of private voluntary organizations (PVOs) after the 1976 earthquake.* Many of these relief organizations decided to stay in the highlands even after the main reconstruction work was complete. All but a few of these groups greatly reduced their operations during the bloodshed of the Lucas Garcia regime (1978-82).

Starting in 1982, a second wave of PVOs arrived in the highlands. They were mostly fundamentalist and

---

* There are two broad categories of PVOs: international PVOs and national ones. International PVOs generally receive some support from their home governments in the form of direct funding, food supplies, or transportation aid. AID funds U.S. PVOs in two ways: 1) through general support grants from the Washington office and 2) through operation or program grants from the national AID Mission. Most PVOs depend on both types of support. National or indigenous PVOs also often receive AID support. Dozens of Guatemalan PVOs that work through the military-tied CRN receive AID funds through counterpart or local currency agreements with the government.

right-wing humanitarian groups attracted by the evangelicalism of Rios Montt (member of the Church of the Word, a branch of the California church Gospel Outreach) and the opportunities presented by the incipient pacification plan. The Church of the Word led the influx of evangelical churches. Church elder Alfred Kaltsschmidt in 1983 said, "We cannot deny that we have worked in coordination with the army and against the guerrillas."[40]

The Christian Broadcasting Network (CBN), headed by Pat Robertson, sponsored a campaign to send money and agricultural and medical technicians to help design the first model villages of the Rios Montt pacification program.[41] The Foundation of Aid to the Indian People (FUNDAPI), another fundamentalist organization, became active in the Ixil Triangle at the height of the counterinsurgency campaign. FUNDAPI was founded in September 1982 by the Summer Linguistics Institute/Wycliffe Bible Translators (evangelical organization that translates the Bible into local languages), the Carroll Behrhorst Foundation (a medical clinic in Chimaltenango operated by a doctor from Tulane University and aligned with the military), and Church of the Word. FUNDAPI's medical aid and bilingual education programs came with an ardently anticommunist and pro-government message.

Supplies for early pacification work came from Love Lift International, the relief arm of Gospel Outreach. Rios Montt had selected Love Lift International "to coordinate the involvement of Christian ministries and churches throughout the United States in relief and development projects" in Guatemala. Love Lift International funding came from such U.S. evangelical figures as Pat Robertson and Lorin Cunningham of Youth with a Mission.[42] Congressman Jack Kemp also supported this effort.

Pacification supplies also came from the Air Commandos, an organization of former or current members of Special Forces units. Retired General Harry Aderholt, the chief figure in the Air Commandos, claimed that it delivered $10 million to the development poles. Its personnel in Guatemala met regularly with the military to arrange storage and transport of its supplies. The Air Commandos operate a medical clinic in the town of Nebaj in the Ixil Triangle. The clinic's staff, who live in the army's outpost in Nebaj, depend for most of their medical supplies on World Medical Relief, another right-wing U.S. group.[43] In the United States, the Air Commandos work closely with the National Defense Council, CBN, Knights of Malta, and the World Anti-Communist League.

Harris Whitbeck, a shadowy figure with close connections in the Guatemalan military and right wing, was one of the first proponents of using international humanitarian aid in connection with the country's pacification program. Born in the United States and a former U.S. Marine, Whitbeck has lived for many years in Guatemala and holds Guatemalan citizenship. During the Rios Montt regime, he served as the president's close adviser and public relations officer.

Whitbeck, a director of the Behrhorst Foundation, arranged for military transport and support of the humanitarian aid from CBN and FUNDAPI. He is also influential in Partners of the Americas, which promotes business and social ties between the state of Alabama and Guatemala. Partners of the Americas depended on the participation of Robert Culbertson, who was Guatemala's AID director in 1970. Culbertson said that not only did the PVO establish business connections but that it also served as a "channel for those who are worried about the dangers of communism in this hemisphere."[44] Together with the Behrhorst Foundation and Summer Institute of Linguistics, the Partners of Americas submitted a joint proposal to AID in 1982 to provide emergency relief for Indians in the areas of conflict.[45]

The latest of Harris Whitbeck's ventures in the highlands is a voluntary organization known as PAVA (Program to Help the Residents of the Altiplano). PAVA--which originally called itself PAVVA or the Program to Assist the Victims of Violence in the Altiplano--maintains a rocky relationship with the AID Mission in Guatemala. But it has received at least two AID grants for its relief work in Huehuetenango (in the development pole of Chacaj), Chimaltenago and other areas of the highlands. It coordinates its work with CRN. Since 1983, PAVA claims to have distributed food, clothes, medicine, and tools to over 87,000 victims of the "disturbances" who came from 122 highlands villages. Like the military, PAVA concentrates its "community development projects" in communities "severely affected by the violence."46 Whitbeck, who boasts of powerful contacts in Washington, arranged for the grants directly with AID in Washington rather than with the local AID Mission. In a 1984 interview, Whitbeck praised the counterinsurgency tactics of the army:

> Just several years ago, it seemed as if the entire Altiplano belonged to the communists. Most of the Indians were with the guerrillas. I know because I almost got shot when I landed in a helicopter once. But now things have calmed down. The army is up there handing out food and helping the people. It's really hard anymore to distinguish the soldiers from the social workers.47

Another major figure in PAVA is Dennis Wheeler, a former Peace Corps volunteer who has remained in Guatemala as a entrepreneur with interests in agriculture, crafts, and a prominent bar in Antigua. Ever since Wheeler began working as a Peace Corp volunteer over 15 years ago in the Peten province, he has maintained a close working relationship with the military. In addition to his work with PAVA, Wheeler is involved in colonization and non-traditional agro-export projects intended to benefit highlands Indians. In a 1983 letter to raise funds for PAVA, Dennis Wheeler called General Rios Montt "a man of honor and integrity."[48]

During the Rios Montt regime, both the U.S. and Guatemalan governments began to encourage the return of more traditional PVOs to the highlands. But most of them expressed reluctance at renewing operations in the Altiplano either because they feared continued violence or because they wanted to avoid any contribution to the government's pacification campaign. By 1985, exclusive of the evangelicalists and right-wing groups, only a handful of PVOs were active in the Altiplano.

In its 1986 Country Development Strategy Statement, AID stated that it was still "encouraging the re-entry of PVOs into the highlands." AID said that the PVOs would participate in programs that "address Guatemala's development priorities." Similarly, AID also supported the return of Peace Corps volunteers to the highlands.

An official of the Salvation Army said that in 1984 AID actually pressured the organization to work in the highlands. AID's petitions to the Salvation Army were repeatedly turned down at the lower levels of the organization but the National Board finally acceded, bowing to the argument that they could not refuse to aid Guatemalans simply because of politics. "But they don't see the other side," remarked this Salvation Army representative. "They don't understand that it's just as political to be giving aid."[49]

Like the Salvation Army, Project Hope was enlisted by AID to assist in the care of displaced persons in the highlands. Under the supervision of the army, Project

Hope assists refugees with housing, health care, and other basic needs. In addition to its work among the displaced, Project Hope manages an "integrated rural development" project in San Marcos in the western highlands. Project Hope worked with PAVA on a needs assessment for the highlands—a study that has greatly assisted AID and the Guatemalan military in targeting pacification projects.

The largest PVO operating in Guatemala is CARE, which distributes PL480 Title II food in areas of conflict. CARE food goes to the population within the development poles through its Mother and Infant Care program and various food-for-work projects. It is most prominent in the development pole of Playa Grande in the Franja Transversal del Norte, where it distributes food to about 6,000 families and manages a non-traditional agro-export production project that grows cardamom. CARE has cooperated closely with AID and the Guatemalan army in Playa Grande. Rejecting criticism that CARE is part of the pacification effort, Christian Nill of the CARE office in Guatemala City said, "We try to do our own work in Quiche and Huehuetenango because it is where the poorest people are."[50]

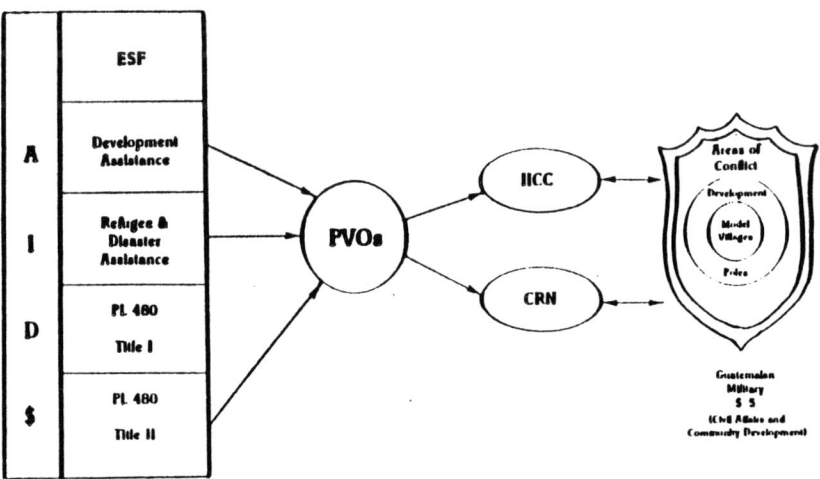

Another PVO active in Guatemala is the Penny Foundation--known in Guatemala as Fundacion del Centavo (FUNDACEN). Created in the 1960s with funds from the AID-backed Pan American Development Foundation, it works in the highlands with the AID Commercial Land Markets Project which encourages the landless and small farmers to use AID financing to buy parcels purchased from larger landholders. Catholic Relief Services (CRS) also works in Guatemala, but has tried to keep its operations relatively separate from AID and military projects. CRS director in Guatemala Dan Moriarty said in 1985 that CRS has not followed up on AID's repeated requests to work on new AID projects in the highlands "because AID works with the military."[51] But CRS does distribute PL480 food, and CRS officials acknowledge that the military sometimes obligates it to use the food in ways that complement counterinsurgency efforts.

A key PVO organization in Guatemala is ASINDES (Association of Non-Governmental Institutions), a Guatemalan organization founded in 1981 to coordinate the work of PVOs. At that time the purpose of ASINDES was to protect PVOs from army violence by acting as their official voice before the military government. Its new role is to act as the collective financial agent for small PVOs operating in the country. ASINDES director Hugo Figuero said the organization is pushing private-enterprise development. The Inter-American Foundation (IAF), a semi-autonomous organization entirely backed by U.S. government funding, has been its principal donor but AID is expected to begin funding ASINDES in 1986.[52]

PVOs play a crucial role in pacification, particularly through intelligence gathering. The right-wing and evangelical PVOs have helped the military spread its message of anticommunism and loyalty to the state. PVOs like PAVA provide information to AID and the military about the location of refugees and the extent of the damage caused by the army's counterinsurgency violence. The army has used this type of information to plan its development poles and model villages. Both AID and the army rely on information gathered by PVOs--such as population counts, health surveys, and needs assessments--to target their pacification aid and so-called development programs. Like AID itself, PVOs also supply the technical assistance and planning and distribution skills that the Guatemalan military lacks.

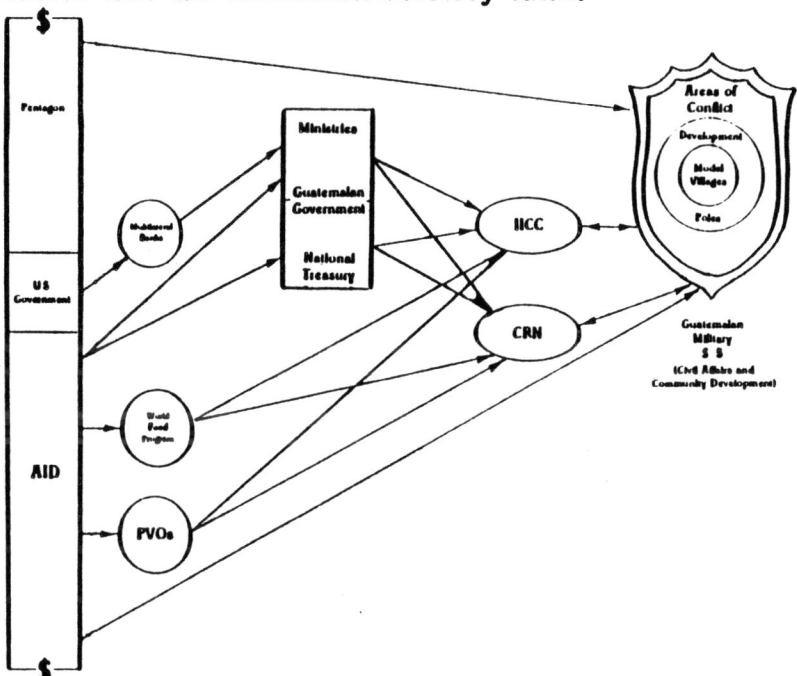

ASSISTANCE FROM ISRAEL AND TAIWAN

Besides the United States, the Guatemalan military has been able to count on assistance from two other countries in its activities in the highlands. Israel and Taiwan have both provided Guatemala ample help in the planning and execution of pacification.

Israeli assistance to Guatemala can be traced back to the late 1970s when high-placed Guatemalan officials began traveling to Israel and working with Israeli advisers. One such trip to Israel included Colonel Fernando Castillo Ramirez, director of the National Cooperative Institute (INACOP), who was interested in learning how to use cooperatives to defuse rural tension. Joining Ramirez was Leonel Giron, the director of colonization programs in the Franja Transversal del Norte. Soon afterwards, Israeli advisers arrived in Guatemala to help plan civic action programs designed to pacify the Indian population in the explosive Ixcan area of northern Quiche.[53]

In 1978, the International Cooperation Division of Israel's Foreign Ministry initiated a program that issued grants to Guatemalan officials to study cooperatives and rural development. Under that program, officials from the national Agricultural Development Bank (BANDESA), the General Directorate of Agrarian Services (DIGESA), and the National Institute of Agrarian Transformation (INTA) received instruction in Israel.

Advice and planning about controlling and resettling hostile population groups have also come from Israel. Among the military and the right wing in Guatemala, talk about the "Palestinization" of the Indian population became common in the early 1980s.[54] In practice, this has meant development and resettlement programs modeled after Israel's programs in the occupied lands of the West Bank. During the Lucas regime, Guatemalan visitors to Israel were particularly interested in the Rehovot land settlement center in the West Bank area:

> Here were workable models of rural development which avoided the need for agrarian reform. Colonization projects in the occupied territories were carried out under strict military supervision, expressly designed to colonize and redevelop infertile

lands, often clashing with the wishes of a hostile local population. Some elements of the Israeli kibbutz and the cash-crop moshav found their way into Lucas Garcia's abortive "Integrated Plan for Rural Communities."[55]

Guatemalan Air Force Colonel Eduardo Wohlers, former director of CRN, credited the training that he and other officers received in Israel with the success of pacification in Guatemala. "Many of our technicians are Israeli-trained," said Wohlers. "The model of the kibbutz is planted firmly in the minds of my officials. I think it would be fascinating to turn our highlands into that kind of system."[56]

Wohlers invoked the positive image of the Israeli kibbutz to describe Guatemala's model villages, an entirely different kind of rural organization. But there is little similarity between the voluntary cooperativism of the kibbutz and the forced resettlement programs in Guatemala's development poles. In the model villages, the Guatemalan military has tried to institute purportedly cooperative structures like community kitchens, meeting places, and educational activities. But rather than encouraging independent communal development, the military uses these new institutions to break down the Indian culture and to re-educate them.

Guatemala's pacification strategists envision a total agrarian transformation of the highlands that would integrate Indian communities into national economic life while making them less susceptible to guerrilla propaganda. Along with AID rural development experts, advisers from Israel have fired that vision and provide the technical assistance in irrigation and vegetable production. Wohlers said the army seeks "the definitive transformation of the face of the Indian highlands. We foresee huge plantations of fruit and vegetables, with storage and processing plants. We aim to put in the entire infrastructure for frozen broccoli, Chinese cabbage, watermelon...a total of fifteen new export crops."[57]

Taiwan, which has the second-largest diplomatic mission in Guatemala, also supports nontraditional agroexport development in Indian communities in the highlands. Explaining why his country was supporting Guatemala with generous economic and military aid, I Chen Loh, Taiwan's ambassador to Guatemala, said, "We believe that it is necessary to help those who want to resist the spread of communism."[58] Both El Salvador and Guatemala have relied on Taiwan for instruction in psychological operations. General Rodolfo Lobos Zamora, chief of staff under Mejia Victores, praised Taiwanese advisers as being "specialists in psychological warfare."[59] The operations of the World Anti-Communist League (WACL) also link Taiwan and Guatemala. WACL, which was jointly founded by Taiwan and South Korea, has been closely associated with Guatemala's death squads.

Israel, and to a lesser extent Taiwan, have served as proxies for the United States in Guatemala. At a time when congressional restrictions blocked military aid to Guatemala, this aid came from Israel. In 1981, both countries signed a Memorandum Concerning Strategic Cooperation Between the United States and Israel. Part one of this memorandum concerned joint military cooperation "outside the east Mediterranean zone" and the third part called for arms sales to "third parties."[60] Secretary of State Alexander Haig admitted in 1981 that the U.S. government explicitly requested Israel to help Guatemala, and U.S. officials have acknowledged a "convergence of interests" in Central America.[61] A 1983 Washington Post article quoted Israeli officials as saying that they "would be willing to act as a U.S. proxy in areas where congressional restraints or human rights concerns raise obstacles to direct U.S. aid."[62]

In April 1985, another proxy agreement was signed between the United States and Israel that allows AID to allocate funds to Israel for agribusiness development projects in the third world. The funds are channeled to Israel's Division of International Cooperation and the country's Center for International Cooperation for Agricultural Development. When asked about Israeli-U.S. cooperation in third world countries, Yehuda Ben-Me'ir, Deputy Foreign Minister in the Shamir government, said:

> It is not secret that there are agreements for U.S.-Israeli cooperation in Asian countries, Africa, Latin America, and Central America. The United States has interests throughout the world. Israel has its own interests in the countries of the world. In some places these interests overlap and the two countries cooperate.[63]

SIMILARITIES BETWEEN U.S. ECONOMIC AID PROJECTS AND THE ARMY'S SECURITY AND DEVELOPMENT PLAN

U.S. Economic Aid	Military Pacification

COLONIZATION

1. In 1976, AID disbursed over $5 million for a pilot colonization scheme in the Franja Transversal del Norte that involved resettling landless peasants from other areas of the country in 50 model sites centered in the Ixcan and Playa Grande region of northern Quiche. The mineral and oil resources of the Franja Transversal del Norte were a prime reason for AID's and the Guatemalan government's particular interest in expanding the region's social and physical infrastructure. The colonization project called for the construction of roads into this isolated region and for new schools and clinics. The military and the Institute for Agrarian Transformation (INTA) have used AID funds to build 4 times as many roads as were originally planned, thereby diverting funds scheduled for schools and clinics. AID has proposed to greatly expand the Franja Transversal colonization project with a $13.2 million Franja Transversal Development project. The goal of this project is to improve the "social and political stability" of this region by settling more families and "establishing geographic poles of agricultural development." AID says that the "next logical step after settling the Franja Transversal is to push

1. The Ixcan/Playa Grande area was the original stronghold of the EGP guerrillas and the site of its first military action in 1975. The colonization project coincided with the army's interests in two ways. First, the project increased military access to guerrilla bases and created a social infrastructure to control the population. Second, the project opened up this region to exploitation by the military elite. Settlers were used to clear land but were later pushed off their farms to make way for ranches owned by generals. In collaboration with INTA, generals like Romeo Lucas Garcia gained title to vast stretches of the Franja Transversal del Norte (known in Guatemala as the "Zone of the Generals"). The entire colonization project has been incorporated into a development pole.

the frontier into the contiguous Peten"--a new area of guerrilla insurgency.
AID Projects:
Small Farmer Development
Small Farmer Diversification
New Lands Settlement
Cardamom Cultivation
Franja Development (proposed)

ELECTRICITY

2. In 1979, a time when the army was escalating its rural counterinsurgency campaign, AID began an $8 million rural electrification project. In 1982, AID renewed the program, specifying that the funds be used in the highlands. A 1985 report by AID said one of the reasons for the increased budget of the electrification project was that INDE (the military-controlled institute of electricity) had selected more isolated highlands villages for electrification. AID funds INDE's Human Resettlement Institute, which manages model villages populated by Indians pushed off their lands by new hydroelectric plans in Quiche and Alta Verapaz.
AID Projects:
Rural Electrification II
INDE Rural Promoters

2. While only 25 percent of rural Guatemala has electricity, INDE promptly brought rural electrification to its new model villages. The army regards electrification as an important step in incorporating the Indians into national life and its Operation Ixil emphasized the importance of electricity in pacification.

RESETTLEMENT

3. AID funded labor-intensive shelter programs in the highlands and projects to resettle refugees who it says were displaced by "the guerrilla war." Survey and monitoring efforts by PVOs were also sponsored by AID. AID has discussed funding the resettlement of refugees in Mexico and has given special attention to the development

3. The resettlement of displaced people is a main reason for the model villages. The army regards the refugees as being past or potential guerrilla supporters and therefore controls all refugee relief programs in the highlands.

pole in Huehuetenango designed to receive refugees returning from Mexico.
AID Projects:
Displaced Persons Resettlement
Disaster Assistance
Secondary Cities and Rural Housing

HOUSING

4. AID has provided materials for low cost "techo minimo" housing in the highlands. In many model villages, the roofing material (aluminum siding known as lamina) has been supplied by AID. At least $500,000 of a counterpart fund established by a 1983 ESF grant was used by the army for "techo minimo" shelter supplies for the model villages.
AID Projects:
Displaced Persons Resettlement
Special Development Activities
Community Development Projects

4. The provision of shelter is an essential part of the army's "techo, trabajo, y tortillas" pacification and resettlement program. The army used CRN materials and food-for-work programs to have highlands Indians build model villages and resettlement camps.

ROADS

5. At least 40 percent of AID's total development assistance has been dedicated to rural road construction and maintenance in the highlands and Franja Transversal del Norte.
AID Projects:
Small Farmer Diversification
Highlands Agriculture Development
Farm-to-Market Roads
Franja Development (proposed)

5. Roadbuilding has been a boon to the army's pacification plan in that it keeps large numbers of potential guerrillas employed and fed while providing better access to remote guerrilla strongholds. Operation Ixil specifically mentions expanding the network of roads in northern Quiche and food-for-work labor.

WATER

6. AID funds most new construction of potable water and sanitation systems in the highlands and pays for the rural promoters and PVOs that work with CRN.
AID Projects:
Rural Potable Water

6. The extension of water and sanitation services in the development poles has been an important drawing card in the army's attempts to convince people of the benefits offered by living in the model villages so close to the army.

Water Development
Water and Sanitation II
Water, Women, and Health

HEALTH

7. Under several programs, AID is training over 3,000 Guatemalan "promoters" to work in rural areas to improve health and sanitation. In 1984, AID funded two-thirds of the budget of the government's Department of Health Services and paid for the construction of all the country's rural healthposts.
AID Projects:
Community Based Health
Health Outreach
Rural Health Promoters

7. Army plans call for each of the model villages and resettlement centers to have health posts, although most of them have no doctors and only disburse aspirin and outdated medicine.

AGRICULTURE

8. AID has advocated that small farmers start producing vegetables for export. AID states that the project will "improve economic well-being of rural people living in the northwestern Highlands." AID-funded agronomists and extension agents are called in by the army to assist in agriculture planning for the model villages.
AID Projects:
Small Farmer Diversification
Highlands Agriculture Development
Commercial Land Markets
Small Farmer Marketing
Rural Promoters
Agribusiness Development

8. The government thinks that incorporating Indian farmers into an export market will make them more dependent on government programs, thereby reducing their susceptibility to guerrilla influence. The army opposes agrarian reform but, like AID, supports land titling, colonization, and commercial land sales projects that receive international assistance. Operation Ixil specifically mentioned the goal of "diversifying cultivation" and army personnel talk of eradicating the "culture of corn" among the Indians of the highlands.

CREDIT

9. AID is the main contributor to BANDESA, the country's rural credit institution, which makes it the largest source of credit for small farmers.
AID Projects:
Small Farmer Marketing

9. Operation Ixil recommended the establishment of offices of BANDESA near the model villages. BANDESA provides credit for the development of the model villages and the agricultural projects associated with them.

Rural Enterprises
Highlands Agriculture
  Development
Small Farmer Diversification

COOPERATIVES

10. In 1979 AID created and has since continued to fund the government-affiliated federation of cooperatives called INACOP to promote rural development, with special emphasis on the highlands and Franja Transversal del Norte.
AID Projects:
Small Farmer Marketing.
Cooperative Strengthening

10. The cooperatives associated with INACOP have been used in development plans in the Altiplano and the Franja Transversal del Norte. Operation Ixil included among its objectives the nationalization of several large estates in the area and the formation of cooperatives under the guidance of INACOP to manage the lands. The plan also recommended the establishment of new cooperatives in the model villages. The army has outlawed cooperatives not closely associated with the government for being "Marxist-inspired."

EDUCATION

11. AID funds programs to improve the rural education for monolingual Mayan language speaking Indians through its Castellanizacion (Spanish language program) Program. AID also trains the program's outreach workers and educators.
AID Projects:
Rural Primary Education
Non-Formal Education
Education Administration
Bilingual Education

11. The army encourages the spread of bilingual education in the highlands because it feels that if the Indians learn Spanish they will fit into the dominant society better. In 1982, the army asked the Guatemalan evangelical organization FUNDAPI to set up bilingual instruction programs with an anticommunist message in the Ixil Triangle. In its section on Public Education, Operation Ixil included "the promotion of bilingual education," "the construction of more schools," and "the preparation of new programs that include at least 50 percent of education in issues of civic action and the strengthening of ideology."

CARE

12. In conjunction with CARE, AID is trying to create a development base in the Playa Grande development pole by having settlers grow and sell cardamom. CARE also distributes PL480 food in development poles.
AID Project:
Cardamom Cultivation

12. CARE works with the army's Civil Affairs and CRN in development poles, particularly at Playa Grande.

FORESTRY

13. AID funds provide a major source of funding for such ministries as INAFOR (National Forestry Institute) and INFOM (Municipal Development Institute) which have increased their operations in the highlands. AID funding for INAFOR is a main source of food-for-work projects.
AID Project:
Small Farmer Diversification

13. The army has commissioned INAFOR to clear sites for model villages and new roads.

COMMUNITY DEVELOPMENT

14. AID's funding of INFOM (which AID created) was originally scheduled to develop towns damaged by the 1976 earthquake but many of these funds are now being used as part of the reconstruction work resulting from the counterinsurgency war.
AID Project:
Municipal Development

14. The army has used funds and technical expertise from INFOM to create town centers and administrative structures in the development poles.

Guatemala: What Next?

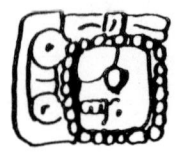

The inauguration of Christian Democrat Vinicio Cerezo Arevalo as Guatemala's new president in January 1986 marked the beginning of a new stage in the country's political process. The U.S. government took part from the beginning: AID directly supported the election process, paying for the ballot paper and for the training of electoral personnel by the Supreme Election Tribunal and the Center for Political Studies (CEDEP). The Reagan Administration hailed Cerezo's election as another success story in the U.S.-supported democratization of Central America while at the same time calling for expanded economic assistance and renewed military aid once a civilian president took office.

The widespread popular support in Guatemala for Cerezo demonstrated rejection of military rule and the right-wing parties. Many regarded Cerezo's candidacy as the very last chance for peaceful reform in Guatemala. Cerezo promised "to fashion a new country," but many doubt his ability to follow through with that promise and also wonder to what extent he will really try.[1] At the time of Cerezo's inauguration, the newly constituted Forum of Guatemalans in Exile said that the country "needs and demands profound economic, social, and political changes as a fundamental condition for attempting the transition to democracy." But this organization of intellectual, political, and union leaders has warned that these changes are impossible when the rabid politics of counterinsurgency still dominate the country.

Like the military, Washington supported democratization as necessary to maintain internal political stability in Guatemala. A stable Guatemala also would be beneficial to U.S. business. In June 1986, the hopeful attitude of corporate America was reflected in an awards function in New York, where the Society of the Americas, an influential group of U.S. entrepreneurs, presented Cerezo with its Golden Insignia award.

Both U.S. business and the Reagan Administration consider democratization as a way to expand U.S. influence in all sectors through the use of military and economic aid programs. The Guatemalan military saw the elections as part of the democratization of the country, but within predetermined boundaries. As early as 1982, the military had called for constituent-assembly and presidential elections as part of its pacification strategy. Elections could reduce the appeal of the guerrillas, improve the country's international image, reduce popular discontent, and attract foreign aid.

In a report on Guatemala in 1985, the British Parliamentary Group on Human Rights pinpointed the military's motives in permitting elections:

> The first point to underline is that if the military succeeded in creating a kind of democratic facade behind which they can continue to manipulate the levers of power, then they would have acquired some international credibility and that could be very important to them in obtaining foreign aid, foreign investment, and political benefits....[2]

THE ECONOMIC NIGHTMARE

As economic problems worsened after 1982, the military recognized that elections could free it of the headaches of managing the country's dismal finances.

When Mejia Victores stepped down, the state of the economy had never been worse. Since 1982, the country had suffered negative economic growth. Exports were 25 percent below the 1980 level, and the foreign debt had increased from $1 billion in 1980 to $2.5 billion in 1986. In 1980, debt servicing as a percent of exports was 7 percent; by 1985 debt servicing hogged 40 percent of export income.

The poor have been hit the hardest by the decline. About 75 percent of Guatemalans live in poverty, and 40 percent cannot afford a minimum diet. By 1985, at least 45 percent of the economically active population did not have full-time or permanent jobs. Between 1970 and 1984, the share of income enjoyed by the top 20 percent of the population increased from 47 to 57 percent, while the poorest 20 percent saw their share of income drop from 7 to 5 percent.3

Upon taking office, Cerezo had to face this economic nightmare. While he can count on increased financial assistance, the prospects are not good for attracting the immense sums of international funds the economy requires. And by promising not to sponsor any substantial reforms, Cerezo has limited his options for improving the situation.

Despite Cerezo's reluctance, many organizations are taking advantage of the political opening his presidency represents. Only four days into his term, thousands of landless Guatemalans poured into suburban areas, built makeshift huts, and demanded government aid. In April 1986, over 10,000 campesinos marched from Escuintla in the south to Guatemala City. They asked that the government sell to them at an accessible price three state-owned farms mortgaged to the Bank of America. President Cerezo has since acceded to this demand.

Two strikes in April 1986 were followed by the first May Day demonstration in Guatemala since 1980. The

Guatemalan Confederation of Union Unity (CUSG), which has connections with the AFL-CIO, backed out of the May Day celebrations to initiate its own event that honored Cerezo. Despite the pullout of the CUSG, more than 5,000 people from a variety of unions participated.

The biggest thorn in Cerezo's side has been the Mutual Support Group (GAM), a well-organized and persistent human rights organization that has been persecuted by military and paramilitary forces. The GAM has garnered a great deal of international support for its demand that Cerezo begin a process in which those responsible for the recent and past violence be brought to justice. Cerezo has held the group at bay, saying that the prosecution of military officers for past atrocities would be "suicidal."

Human rights activists, workers, and campesinos are expected to exert steady pressure on the Cerezo administration for improvement in human rights, better wages, and more equitable land distribution. In a country where 1 percent of the landholders own 34 percent of the land (much of which is idle), agrarian reform would improve income distribution, increase internal purchasing power, and reduce the need to import food.

Another needed reform is the restructuring of the tax system. The country's tax income as a percentage of its GDP (Gross Domestic Product) is one of the lowest in the world. In 1983, it was only 5.3 percent of the GDP (down from 9.7 percent in 1979), while elsewhere in Central America the percentage ranges from 11 to 22 percent. The other main characteristic of the country's tax structure is that over 80 percent of taxes are indirect taxes on goods and services, while only 20 percent comes from direct taxes on income and wealth.[4]

The country's elite has opposed the raising of direct taxes. Rather than risk the ire of the oligarchy, the government will probably raise indirect taxes that fall disproportionately on consumers. Nationalization of foreign trade and banking is a reform measure that would give the government more control over the economy. This would stop the loss of foreign exchange resulting from the hoarding of dollars by exporters in international banks.

These and other possible reforms were ruled out even before Cerezo took office by the leading powerbrokers and their business organizations. His economic policy is constrained by his own financial advisers, who come from the conservative wing of the Christian Democrats and are closely tied to the major agroexporters, bankers, and industrialists.

The centerpiece of Cerezo's economic policy, the National, Social and Economic Reordering Program, does not differ greatly from that of General Mejia Victores. The program calls for elimination of the parity that the quetzal has maintained with the U.S. dollar for 60 years. Only one transaction will remain at parity: the payment of foreign debt.

Even the U.S.-supported CUSG, a staunch supporter of Cerezo, criticized the Reordering Program for lacking adequate salary increases and credit assistance for small-scale producers. Other organizations objected to the large concessions made to the economic elite at the expense of the majority sectors.

The conservative economic position of the government is bolstered by the proposals of the United States and of the International Monetary Fund. Rather than use its influence to encourage reforms, AID advocates reduced government control, more incentives for the private sector, and an expanded emphasis on agroexports. The United States also backs the IMF's demands for currency devaluation, cuts in government spending and employment, and increased taxes on consumers.

AID STEPS INTO THE NATIONAL PALACE

AID intends to use its increased economic assistance as leverage for reform in Guatemala. Not for the kind of social reforms that the Arbenz government tried to initiate or the ones advocated by peasant and worker organizations but reforms aimed to benefit the private sector, particularly the agroexporters. In recent years, AID has attempted to mold the economy in line with the policies of the Reagan Administration and the recommendations of the Kissinger Commission. Since the elections, higher levels of economic assistance to Guatemala have increased AID's ability to dictate economic and political policy in the country.

In its Policy Dialogue Plan for 1986-87, AID states that in the past several years it has carried out a structure policy dialogue with officials at every level of the military government from "authorities at the highest central government level" to those "at regional government levels through formal briefings and program discussions with departmental governors [who were appointed by the military], military commanders, and members of the departmental coordinating committees."5 But it said that it has previously lacked the leverage to condition its aid on its policy recommendations.

In coming years, AID intends to demand policy reforms as a condition for the release of its assistance. Such reforms would include a cutback in public spending, currency devaluation, higher gasoline prices, higher taxes, an increased focus on rural development, increased incentives for the private sector, and support for IMF austerity measures.

AID is taking care not to alienate the Guatemalan oligarchy. In fact, it has designed its projects to coincide with the interests of the oligarchy. The AID mission notes that agrarian reform is "an unacceptable concept in present-day Guatemala." Instead, it promises that discussions and negotiations will be pursued with the private sector before it proceeds with the Commercial Land Markets projects in which AID intends to use private sector credit institutions as the channel for land sales financing. Similarly, its Agribusiness Development project will seek joint ventures between U.S. investors and the local private sector. Like its other agricultural development projects, this new AID project aims to increase nontraditional export production in the highlands. AID is also putting $10 million into a Private Sector Project to increase credit and opportunities for the business community.

Guatemala is the chief focus of the new Central America Peace Scholarships project which was recommended by the Kissinger Commission. The principal purpose of this program is to "promote democratic processes and counter a high level of Soviet Bloc [educational] efforts." The scholarship program is bringing hundreds of Guatemalan Indians to the United States to learn about the "American way" through instruction at AID-funded programs and educational tours of Washington.

Another new AID initiative in the highlands is the agency's support for a Highland Indian Institute that will aim to create a group of Indian leaders allied to AID and the Guatemalan government. And rather than dealing directly with the major causes of poverty in the highlands, AID has kicked off a population control campaign in Guatemala "with increasing special attention to the indigenous population." The campaign brought criticism from Archbishop Prospero Penados, who stated: "What we are talking about is an incredible sterilization program which is contrary to moral, ethnic, and cultural values."6

Starting in 1985, Guatemala has also received special attention from President Reagan's Democracy Initiative spearheaded by the National Endowment for Democracy (NED). NED is a right-wing organization funded by the United States Information Service to promote U.S. policies and to combat perceived anti-democratic tendencies in third world countries.

Working through new private sector organizations funded by AID, NED has paid for a series of seminars about democracy, communism, and private enterprise. One such seminar hosted by the Camara de Libre Empresa brought Guatemalan and Salvadoran business leaders together to discuss more active private sector participation in politics. NED has also funded a new political think tank called the Center for Political Studies (CEDEP), which acts as a forum between government and the private sector. CEDEP received AID funds to promote the presidential elections. Another NED-funded organization working in Guatemala during the elections was the National Republican Institute for International Affairs which conducted a national political survey aimed to "reinforce the democratic aspirations of the Guatemalan people." NED has also pumped money into labor unions affiliated with the American Institute for Free Labor Development (AIFLD), an organization funded almost entirely by AID to promote conservative trade unions in Latin America.[7]

Other U.S. assistance to Guatemala comes in the form of $25,000 for a Drug Enforcement Agency project and the inclusion of Guatemala in a U.S. anti-terrorism program, which trains police from a number of countries.

HANDS OFF THE MILITARY

During his campaign, Vinicio Cerezo promised to stay within limits defined by the oligarchy and the military. Although he hails from the progressive wing of the Christian Democrats, Cerezo assured the country's elite that his would not be a reformist government. His campaign platform did not differ substantially from the right-wing candidates. He ruled out all social reforms including any type of agrarian reform, saying instead that he supported private sector solutions to the country's serious economic difficulties.

The military has duly warned Cerezo that he must not infringe on their considerable power. As Colonel Edgar Hernandez, regional commander of Alta Verapaz, said:

> The new civilian government will have to respect the Army's hierarchical order and constitutional law....The Army also hopes that the civilian government will respect the military's plans against subversion.[8]

Although there is widespread popular pressure for the prosecution of the military for their leading role in human rights violations, Cerezo announced before his inauguration that he would not proceed with an Argentina-style investigation into military atrocities. Cerezo has, however, disbanded the notorious plainclothes police unit called the Department of Technical Investigations (DIT). By mid-1986, the majority of the police were reincorporated into regular uniformed squads. Because this unit does not fall under military control and has been the subject of complaints from the right wing and private sector as well as human rights groups, it was a relatively safe move for Cerezo to take. Skeptics note that Rios Montt fired hundreds of DIT agents when he took over government in 1982, also proclaiming that this would halt political killings and kidnappings.

The military may have left the National Palace but they still have their hands on the levers of power. Besides their expanded control over civil affairs in the Guatemalan countryside, the military has also been extending its economic control in both the public and private sectors. As an institution, the army has interests in two TV stations and controls the state-owned station; owns a major bank; controls dozens of public corporations including the national airline, the telecommunications company (GUATEL), and the electricity company (INDE). Since 1983 it has, with the assistance of Israel, opened two defense factories, one manufacturing munitions and the other one turning out armored vehicles. The military's latest power grab was to acquire financial control over the international airport in early 1985.[9] In the last three decades, individual army generals have incorporated themselves into the financial elite of Guatemala through their acquisition of vast extensions of land and of major industrial and commercial assets.

Soon after taking office, President Cerezo promised that his government would assert its control over many institutions dominated by the military. But from the beginning of the electoral process the military has clearly warned the civilian candidates that its power was inviolable. That was its condition for turning political power over to civilians. Since the start of the pacification program, the military has a new-found pride in its "military humanism" and "developmentalist" philosophy, and it is unlikely that it will allow the new government to reduce its expanded scope of influence over rural development programs.

Shortly after becoming president, Cerezo declared that the development poles, inter-institutional coordinators and civil patrols were military concepts of development that needed to be overhauled. There has, however been little overhauling. For the most part, the Cerezo government has simply continued the pacification campaign of the military.

President Cerezo and Rene de Leon Schlotter, the new Minister of Urban and Rural Development, each inaugurated new development poles in the first few months of the new government. At the opening of a development pole in Alta Verapaz, Cerezo repeated the pacification rhetoric commonly used by the military. He said:

> For many years the money of the people has been spent on projects which have only benefited the urban population. From this day this will change. The philosophy of the new authorities includes creating a government of the people, for which reason, the government I lead, and which counts on the support of the army and the people which elected it, commits itself to promote a series of projects to benefit the rural area. The Army, the civilian government, teachers, campesinos, and workers, forgetting their differences, must work together in order to live in peace.[10]

Minister Schlotter called the development poles "a fundamental part of the policy of the government to benefit the people." He said that the "principal objective" of his ministry "will be to combat the subversion ideologically, in much the same way as the Army has been doing through the Inter-Institutional Coordination System."[11]

In May 1986, Cerezo retreated from his earlier speeches and stated that the counterinsurgency programs would be maintained as the military had designed them, subject to slight alteration under the development minister. In explaining the continuing support of the civil patrols, which have been accused of human rights abuses, Cerezo said: "It is true that we are not abolishing the civil patrols, but we are working to make them voluntary and to shift their focus to local civic projects."[12]

As for the inter-institutional coordinators, the military seems unconcerned about Cerezo's attempt to introduce more civilians into the structure. Already civilians had been included in the coordination committees, but they had little power. As Colonel Byron Disrael Lima, commander of the military zone in Quiche, said when asked about the possibility of a civilian heading the IIOCs: "We'll still supply the expertise, the machinery, and the manpower." As is commonly acknowledged in Guatemala, the local military commander is the ultimate authority in the countryside.

According to the EGP guerrillas, having a civilian as president of the country will not reduce the power the military exercises through the IIOCs:

> The army certainly is able to turn over the government to civilians but it will not surrender its hegemonic power. It was prepared for this. In this sense, the Inter-Institutional Coordinators are an instrument which permits military power to continue at all levels of government and to continue orientating the budget toward the priorities of counterinsurgency."[13]

The military's definition of democratization--fraud-free constituent assembly and presidential elections--does not cover the extension of civilian control over institutions the military regards as integral to counterinsurgency or essential to its own economic security. The military high command sit secure in the knowledge that President Reagan's concept of democratization does not reach beyond the electoral process. Increased economic and military aid to Guatemala is conditioned only upon the successful conclusion of the electoral process; neither Washington nor Congress have demanded that the military relinquish its power over other institutions as a condition for new assistance.

Cerezo's election has given the Guatemalan security forces access to new resources. Now that Guatemala is "democratized," the country is receiving U.S. military and police aid. Cerezo asked Washington to supply the military with spare parts for helicopters and trucks. Cerezo also accepted a Reagan Administration offer to have U.S. instructors train Guatemalan police in an anti-terrorism program--the first time that the United States has officially trained Guatemalan police since the mid-1970s. Cerezo also made the surprise move of advocating the participation of the armed forces in regional military manuevers. Initially, Cerezo had shown signs of bucking U.S. strategy for regional military and diplomatic unity against Nicaragua. But the call for joint maneuvers and a request that the Central American Defense Council (CONDECA) be reactivated show that Cerezo is willing to cooperate with U.S. strategy in several important ways.

PROSPECTS FOR COUNTERINSURGENCY

A decade ago a popular rebellion surged up the Altiplano accompanied by a new wave of student and labor organizing in the cities. Military repression and oligarchic control of land and income created a massive movement for change. Teachers organized, students held demonstrations, miners marched, workers went out on strike, and peasants demanded more land. At the same time that many Guatemalans were openly declaring their opposition to the military and power elite, guerrillas were organizing a revolutionary armed revolt.

The military viciously struck back. Adopting the standard philosophy of counterinsurgency, the generals set out to break the armed resistance by breaking the links of support that had developed between the guerrillas and the unarmed communities. They have tried to do this through a campaign of indiscriminate terror and through the tactics of pacification and population control.

The Indians of Guatemala paid dearly for their opposition to military and oligarchic rule: Tens of thousands dead, hundreds of villages burned, and hundreds of thousands of rural Guatemalans displaced. A list compiled by the country's Supreme Court in March 1985 showed that the counterinsurgency war had left 120,000 children without parents. A Court official reported privately that the grand total was probably double this figure. Eight out of ten children had lost either a mother or a father and the other two had lost both parents.[14] It is estimated that from 75,000 to 100,000 people died at the hands of the military since 1978. As many as 100,000 Guatemalan refugees now live in Mexico, and the internally displaced are estimated to be as many as 500,000.

The violence reached it height in 1982. Then the army, for the first time, offered the Altiplano Indians something more than repression and fear. Its pacification campaign offered food, work, and shelter to the destitute and displaced. Pacification also included a barrage of psychological operations that placed the blame for the violence on the guerrillas and that charged the rebels with intentionally deceiving the Indians with unrealistic promises of a better life. As a slogan for its pacification efforts, the army added its own name to an international revolutionary slogan: "El ejercito y el pueblo unido, jamas seran vencido." (United, the army and the people will never be defeated.)

The combined campaign of terror and pacification crushed the popular organizations and broke the momentum of the guerrillas. Then the military, under Rios Montt and Mejia Victores, broadened the counterinsurgency strategy. It set in place a number of military-controlled "development" institutions and called for national elections. Altogether, the Guatemalan military has step by step implemented a classic counterinsurgency campaign.

But the fatal flaws in counterinsurgency strategy are now becoming obvious. Army terror has failed to dislodge the guerrillas, who have in the last couple of years regained former strength, increased their military expertise, and expanded their territory of operations. Reported guerrilla actions in 1985 were up over 1983 and 1984, and the area of guerrilla operations has been constantly expanding since the counterinsurgency war was unleashed in the late 1970s. The EGP guerrillas recently have regained strength in highlands communities. And the two other major guerrilla armies, ORPA and FAR, have built strong revolutionary fronts in the southeast provinces and in the vast Peten region.

The pacification program that began with "Beans and Guns" has allowed the army to gain control over the Indian population but it has failed to show any long-term promise. What passes for development are really tactics to maintain control over the population. The military considers humanitarian assistance as a way to achieve political objectives. But this military humanism has not disguised the true identity and purposes of the army. "For years, they have stolen our sons to be soldiers, and our daughters for pleasure," noted one elderly Ixil Indian. "It will take more than beans to atone for that history."15

The food distribution and work programs--the drawing cards of pacification--have proved to be temporary solutions to deep-seated problems. Once the roads and model villages are built, there is no more work, and consequently no food. In the model villages, Indian families sit in their new electrified techo minimo homes with no food, no work, and no plots to farm. Instead of improving, conditions are worsening in these target areas. Corn production is down, and residents earn less income because members of the civil patrol cannot easily leave their communities to find seasonal work on coastal plantations.

Not wanting to tackle the economic inequities in Guatemala, the military has turned to foreign-designed development strategies like non-traditional agroexport production that leave historical oligarchic structures intact. Those agroexport development strategies advocated by the army and AID do not offer any real promise for the poor. Nontraditional crops are not suitable for most of the mountainous highlands, and the majority of Indian farmers have neither enough land nor resources to risk cultivating crops that do not have a secure market and which they do not eat. Completed model villages like Acul and Acamal have been unable to produce marketable quantities of nontraditional cash crops, let alone surpluses in staple goods like corn and beans.

In the name of development, the Indians have seen pacification measures designed to increase "security," not to develop the region in their interests. The only visible development in the development poles are roads and the so-called model villages.

The national elections succeeded in stabilizing Guatemala by improving its international image, opening up new sources of foreign financing, and assuaging internal discontent. But this will only be a temporary stability given the tremendous economic problems faced by the Cerezo government and the constraints imposed on the government by the military, oligarchy, AID, and the IMF.

Without true development and without major reform, the prospects for pacification are dim. The civil defense patrols, scorched earth tactics, and increased military presence in isolated areas have hindered the guerrillas movement's efforts to forge close ties with rural communities. But in the last couple of years, the guerrillas have shown a new strength and tactical sophistication.

In pursuing its strategy of counterinsurgency--whose three major elements are terror, pacification, and democratization--the military has demonstrated its efficiency and sophistication. While it has pulled off a textbook-style counterinsurgency campaign, the Guatemalan military has neither destroyed the insurgency nor eliminated the roots of rebellion.

REFERENCE NOTES

AFTER THE COUP: DESIGNING THE SHOWCASE

1. Stephen Schlesinger and Stephen Kinzer, Bitter Fruit: The Untold Story of the American Coup in Guatemala (New York: Doubleday, 1982).
2. Guatemala: Elections 1985 (Guatemala City: Inforpress Centroamericana, October 1985), p. 4.
3. See The Wall Street Journal, June 14, 1984 for an account of this period.
4. Freda Kirchway, "Guatemala Guinea Pig," The Nation, July 10, 1954.
5. Susanne Jonas and David Tobis, Guatemala, (Berkeley: NACLA, 1974), p. 44.
6. Foreign Assistance and Related Agencies Appropriations for 1968, Hearings Before a Subcommittee of the Committee on Appropriations, Part 2, Economic Assistance, House of Representatives, 1967, p. 379. See fascinating first hand account of AID failures in Central America in We Don't Know How: An Independent Audit of What They Call Success in Foreign Assistance, by William and Elizabeth Paddock, (Ames: Iowa State University Press, 1973).
7. Charles Hillinger, "Guatemala Booms Under New Rule," Los Angeles Times, June 30, 1957.
8. Susanne Jonas, Guatemala: Plan Piloto Para El Continente, (San Jose: Educa, 1981), p. 205.
9. U.S. Aid to Guatemala, (Guatemala: United States Information Service, 1959), p. 6.
10. See "Dr. Klein and the Klein Doctrine," Latin American Report, October 1958, p. 22. Cited in Jonas p. 206.
11. George Ball, "Telegram to all American Diplomatic Posts in Central America, Caracas, Mexico, Panama, and Santo Domingo," January 5, 1963. Quoted in Gordon L. Bowen, "U.S. Policy Toward Guatemala 1954-1963," Armed Forces & Society, Winter 1984, p. 183.
12. Department of State Bureau of Public Affairs, Historical Office, "Historical Study: U.S. Policy Toward Latin America, 1946-1976," June 1975, p. 82. Cited in Bowen, Ibid., p. 184.
13. Bowen, op. cit., p. 168.
14. Bowen, Ibid.
15. John S. Pustay, Major, USAF Counterinsurgency Warfare (New York: The Free Press, 1965) pp. 170-171.
16. Bowen, op. cit., p. 169.
17. Brian Jenkins and Caesar D. Sereseres, "U.S. Military Assistance and the Guatemalan Armed Forces," Armed Forces and Society, August 1977, p. 580.
18. Foreign Assistance and Related Agencies Appropriations for 1968, Hearings Before a Subcommittee of the Committee on

Appropriations, Part 2, Economic Assistance, House of Representatives, 1967, p. 1516.
19. Jenkins and Sereseres, Armed Forces and Society, op.cit., p. 580.
20. Deane Hinton served as Ambassador to El Salvador from 1981 to 1983.
21. Foreign Assistance and Related Agencies Appropriations for 1968, Hearings Before a Subcommittee of the Committee on Appropriations, Part 2, Economic Assistance, House of Representatives, 1967, p. 1515.
22. William and Elizabeth Paddock, We Don't Know How: An Independent Audit of What They Call Success in Foreign Assistance (Ames: Iowa State University Press, 1973).
23. Eduardo Galeano, Guatemala: Occupied Country (New York: Monthly Review, 1967), p. 79.
24. Robert Harris, "Guatemala: Death Squad Disappearances," Amnesty International Information Office, 1975.
25. Time, January 26, 1968.
26. "Prüfen sie die geschichte der menschheit," Der Spiegel, April 1970, which was cited in Brian Jenkins and Caesar D. Sereseres, "U.S. Military Assistance and the Guatemalan Armed Forces," Armed Forces and Society, August 1977, p. 580.

INDIAN REBELLION AND COUNTERINSURGENCY

1. The National Plan of Security and Development was approved by President Rios Montt on April 1, 1982.
2. Junta Militar de Gobierno, Objetivos Nacionales Actuales, March 23, 1982; Estado Mayor General del Ejercito, Plan Nacional de Seguridad y Desarrollo, Anexo H (Ordenes permanentes para el desarrollo de operaciones contrasubversivas) al plan de campana Victoria 82, July 16, 1982. Quoted in George Black, "Under the Gun," NACLA Report on the Americas, November/December 1985, p. 11.
3. Ibid.
4. Ibid.
5. Nancy Peckenham, "Guatemala 1983," (American Friends Service Committee, December 1983), p. 13.
6. U.S. Embassy Information Packet, November 1985.
7. Firmeza 83, "Plan de Trabajo Gubermental."
8. The military added the Civil Affairs and Community Development section to those of Intelligence, Logistics, Operations, and Personnel. Guatemala: Elections 1985, op. cit., p. 33.
9. See George Black, op. cit., p. 12.
10. Development Poles, Polos de Desarrollo, (Guatemala City: Editorial del Ejercito, February 1985), p. 85.
11. Interview by Tom Barry, CRN Executive Secretary Oscar Gallegos, Guatemala City, June 1984.

12. Revista Cultural del Ejercito, Enero-Junio 1985.
13. "Operacion Ixil," Revista Militar, September-December 1982.
14. Development Poles, op.cit., p. 13.
15. Informador Guerrillero, Ano III, No. 36.
16. Ibid.
17. Development Poles, op. cit.
18. Enfoprensa, September 14, 1984; Revista Cultural, op. cit.
19. Interview by Tom Barry with Julio Corsantes, Acamal, June 1984.
20. Interview by Deb Preusch with Isaacs Rodriguez, August 1984.
21. Development Poles, op. cit.
22. Central America Report, January 24, 1986.

PACIFICATION: A JOINT EFFORT

1. Letter from Jay F. Morris, AID, to Senator Patrick J. Leahy, March 6, 1985.
2. Interview by Deb Presuch with Gary Adams, October 1985.
3. "Labor Trends in Guatemala, 1983," Prepared by the American Embassy (Guatemala), p. 6.
4. AID Annual Budget Submission, FY 1984, Guatemala (June 1982), pp. 2-3.
5. Testimony of M. Peter McPherson, Administrator of AID, Subcommittee of Committee on Appropriations, House of Representatives, April 19, 1983, p. 86.
6. Interview by Deb Preusch with Robert Queener, AID, Washington, October 1984.
7. Ibid.
8. Interview by Deb Preusch with Colonel German Grotewald, Guatemala City, August 1984.
9. Interview by Tom Barry with CRN Executive Secretary Oscar Gallegos, Guatemala City, June 1984.
10. Area de Cooperacion Nacional e Internacional de CRN, Informe Anual de Actividades 1984. AID agreement 520-K-036.
11. Ibid.
12. Revista Cultural, Enero-Junio 1985.
13. Interview by Deb Preusch with Colonel Mario Paiz Bolanos, Guatemala City, August 1984.
14. Interview by Deb Preusch with Major-Doctor Luis Sieckavizza, Guatemala City, July 1985.
15. Ibid.
16. Captain John W. Athanson, "Aiding Our Neighbors," Proceedings, February 1985, p. 49.
17. Alvaro Galez, "Ayuda Norteamericana," Prensa Libre, December 20, 1985.
18. Letter to Senator Patrick J. Leahy from Jay F. Morris, AID, March 6, 1985.
19. Foreign Assistance Legislation for FY 86-87, Part 6. Close observers of the Guatemalan military note that the army has consistently refused to use its helicopters for medical

evacuation even when they were available.
20. Press Conference at U.S. Embassy, Guatemala City, December 5, 1985.
21. Ibid.
22. WFP, "Project Summary: Guatemala," Seventeenth Session, 1983.
23. AID, FY 86/87 Action Plan Guatemala, p. 89.
24. Interview by Tom Barry, Guatemala City, source wished to remain unidentified, June 1984.
25. Nancy Peckenham, Guatemala 1983, op. cit., p. 17.
26. Interview by Deb Preusch with Lance Downing, AID's Guatemala Desk Officer, February 1986.
27. Americas Watch, Guatemala: A Nation of Prisoners: Social and Economic Consequences of Repression, January 1984.
28. AID, Highlands Agricultural Development Project.
29. AID, Highlands Agricultural Development Project, p. 4.
30. AID, Small Farmer Development Project, 1984.
31. Judy Van Rest, "AID in Guatemala," Frontlines (Washington: AID), November 1985.
32. Gary Smith, "Abbreviated Economic Analysis of the Small Farmer Development Project," (AID: Office of Rural Development, Report No. 6), May 1983.
33. Interview by Tom Barry with Gary Adams, San Marcos, June 1984.
34. Interview by Tom Barry with Jorge Ramirez, August 1984.
35. Development Poles, op. cit., p. vii.
36. Interview by Deb Preusch, November 1985.
37. Interview by Deb Preusch, November 1985.
38. Interview by Deb Preusch, August 1984.
39. Interview by Deb Preusch, November 1985.
40. Guatemalan Church in Exile, Guatemala, "A New Way of Life": The Development Poles, September/October 1984, p. 9.
41. Shelton H. Davis, "Guatemala: The Evangelical Holy War in El Quiche," The Global Reporter, March 1983.
42. Ibid.
43. Air Commando Newsletter, February 1985, May 1985, August 1985.
44. Jonas, op. cit., p. 352
45. AID, Guatemala project paper: Economic Support Program, January 5, 1983.
46. Fundraising letter from Carmen Torres de Ruiz, President of PAVA, November 1985.
47. Interview by Tom Barry, Antigua, June 1984.
48. Letter was cosigned by Michael Shawcross, another principal figure in PAVA.
49. Interview by Deb Preusch, source wished to remain anonymous, June 1984.
50. Interview by Deb Preusch, August 1984.
51. Interview by Deb Preusch with Dan Moriarty, Guatemala City, December 1985.

52. Interview by Deb Preusch with Dr. Hugo Figuero, Guatemala City, December 1985.
53. Nancy Peckenham, "Bullets and Beans," Multinational Monitor, April 1984; George Black, "Israeli Connection: Not Just Guns for Guatemala," NACLA Report on the Americas, May/June 1983, p. 45.
54. Ibid.
55. George Black, NACLA Report on the Americas, May/June 1983, p. 45.
56. Latin America Regional Report, May 6, 1983; Nancy Peckenham, "Bullets and Beans," Multinational Monitor, April 1984.
57. George Black, NACLA Report on the Americas, May/June 1983, p. 45.
58. Enfoprensa, August 24, 1984.
59. Ibid.
60. Benjamin Beit-Hallahmi, "U.S.-Israeli Central American Connection," The Link, Vol. 18, No. 4, November 1985. The Link is a U.S. journal specializing in Middle Eastern affairs.
61. Ibid.; Miami Herald, May 27, 1984.
62. Washington Post, August 17, 1983.
63. Israeli Foreign Affairs, June 1985.

GUATEMALA: WHAT NEXT?

1. Central America Report, January 17, 1986.
2. Developments in Guatemala and U.S. Options, Hearing before the Subcommittee on Western Hemisphere Affairs of the Committee on Foreign Affairs, House of Representatives, February 20, 1985, p. 2.
3. All economic statistics based on official data summarized in Guatemala: Elections 1985, op. cit., pp. 13-23.
4. Guatemala: Elections 1985, op. cit., p. 15.
5. AID, FY 86/87 Action Plan Guatemala, p. 5.
6. Guatemala Church In Exile, Development: The New Face of War, April 1986.
7. National Endowment for Democracy, Annual Report 1985.
8. Guatemala: Elections 1985, op. cit., p.35.
9. Financial Times, December 7, 1984; Black, NACLA, November-December 1985, op. cit., p. 12.
10. Guatemala Church In Exile, op. cit., p.39.
11. Ibid., p.41.
12. Ibid.
13. Informador Guerrillero, Ano III, No. 36
14. Guatemala: Elections 1985, op. cit., p. 27.
15. Newsweek, December 13, 1982.